COL

BASKETBALL

Jeff Fletcher

Consultant: Dave Hammond

HarperCollins*Publishers*

All photographs courtesy of Allsport except:
Action-Plus Photographic 21, 40, 122, 131, 138, 139, 218. Empics 125, 128. Pete Norton 13, 15, 17, 25, 42, 43, 44, 45, 47, 49, 50, 51, 53, 64, 74, 76, 81, 82, 83, 84, 90, 91, 98, 99, 100, 101, 130, 134, 137, 148, 150, 154, 156, 157, 163, 172, 178, 187, 189, 201, 208, 215, 221, 236, 237. Pete Jenkins/Picturesport Associates Ltd (*Basketball*, A&C Black) 217. Topham 30, 48, 54.
Artwork courtesy of Foundry Arts.

HarperCollins Publishers
PO Box, Glasgow G4 0NB

First published 1999

Reprint 10 9 8 7 6 5 4 3 2 1 0

© The Foundry Creative Media Co. Ltd 1999 (text)

ISBN 0 00472339 2

Created and produced by Flame Tree Publishing, part of The Foundry Creative Media Co. Ltd
Crabtree Hall, Crabtree Lane, Fulham, London SW6 6TY

Printed in Italy by Amadeus S.p.A.

Contents

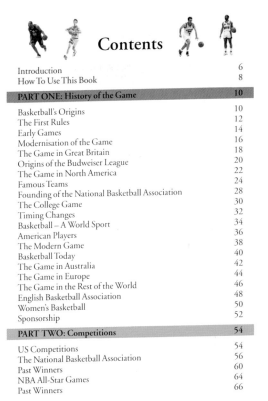

Introduction

Basketball is the fastest-growing sport in the world. Americans have been obsessed with the game for many years, but now basketball has become a truly global sport. Interest in the sport has been increasing steadily in recent decades, but it was the appearance of the United States Dream Team at the 1992 Barcelona Olympics that really caught the public's imagination. Not only did that great side win the gold medal, but it also showed a massive television audience just how magnificent the game could be. Superstars such as Michael Jordan and 'Magic' Johnson became instant heroes to millions of new fans around the world.

Members of the United States Dream Team, Barcelona, 1992.

Pick-up basketball, an impromptu, unscheduled game usually played in public areas, is a social phenomenon in the United States and has developed its own rules, language and indeed fashions. Now this form of basketball is beginning to take root in many other countries outside North America. In Britain, most sports centres and gyms have basketball facilities, and an increasing number of local councils are providing hoops and play areas in public parks and spaces. There are more

basketball clubs and local leagues than ever before and a growing number of schools are adding the game to their sports programmes.

The English Basketball Association has introduced a range of initiatives to help encourage young people to take up the game.

Basketball has come a long way since it was invented just over 100 years ago, and the future for the sport looks extremely healthy.

Chicago Bulls star Michael Jordan.

How To Use This Book

THIS BOOK CONTAINS all the essential information that is needed to play and understand the game of basketball. The origins of the game in the United States are explored, as is the current state of the game there, and this book also looks at the spread of the game to Britain and Europe. The most famous players in the United States and in the rest of the world are given, the backgrounds to the best-known competitions are looked at and current statistics listed. For those who would rather learn how to play the game, and know exactly how take a dunk shot or to play like Shaq O'Neal, there are two comprehensive instruction sections, detailing rules, techniques and tips for the would-be basketball player, or those returning to the sport. A plan of the court is a vital tool to the further understanding of the game; this is given in the rules section. A good level of fitness means that the game can be more enjoyable; fitness tips for players of all ages are given in the section on becoming a player.

Basketball is divided into seven sections, each one dealing with a different aspect of the game, with an extensive Compendium at the end. Each section is colour coded for easy reference. Part One deals with the history of the game, looking back to the origins of basketball. Part Two looks at the competitions in the game, both in the US and in Europe. Part Three looks at the top players in the US and the rest of the world. Part Four is a guide to becoming a player, giving details of kit and equipment needed, where to play and fitness tips. Part Five is a guide to the rules of the game: both a simple overview of the main rules needed by a beginner and a more detailed look at the finer points of the game. Part Six looks at playing the game and gives tips on improving techniques in all aspects of the game: shooting, passing, offence and defence. Part Seven contains information about variations of the game: three-on-three, pick-up, wheelchair and mini basketball.

The Compendium contains a glossary and a list of useful addresses and numbers, such as the English Basketball Association. A comprehensive index will lead you to the relevant information contained in the book.

A The page number appears in a colour-coded box indicating which section you are looking at.

B The aspect of the sport being dealt with is indicated at the head of the appropriate page.

C Instructive, interesting text gives all the essential information needed for the particular aspect of the sport.

D The topic covered on the page will be illustrated with clear photographs or diagrams, with identifying captions where appropriate.

HISTORY OF THE GAME
Basketball's Origins

Basketball is the only popular modern-day sport to have been invented rather than evolving over a period of time. Its inventor, Dr James Naismith, was a Canadian of Scottish extraction who held the post of physical instructor at the School for Christian Workers in Springfield, Massachusetts.

IN 1891, NAISMITH had the task of taking a gym class comprising 18 prospective YMCA general secretaries. Naismith was a prolific sportsman himself: he had played football, American football and professional lacrosse. He was an all-round athlete who enjoyed rugby, boxing, wrestling and canoeing.

The job of keeping his charges occupied in the summer was not difficult, but in the winter the weather prevented the pursuit of outdoor games. Naismith wanted – or rather

Los Angeles Lakers vs. Utah Jazz, 1998.

Naismith originally used peach baskets as his goals; today equipment is much more sophisticated.

his employers required him – to invent a game that would 'be of a recreative nature, something that would appeal to [the men's] play instincts'. He believed it possible to invent a game that would 'be interesting, easy to learn and easy to play'.

From the start, Naismith wanted his game to be played with a large, soccer-type ball, and although in favour of robust games, he needed the game to be relatively safe in an indoor environment. Despite this, however, he was determined that the sport would not be too tame.

The idea of raising the goals was to ensure that to score, players would have to rely on a certain amount of skill and agility, rather than on simple power or strength. Being able to find nothing else, Naismith used peach baskets as his goals. The height of the goals, at 3.05 m (10 ft) was, like the peach basket as a goal, a necessity: 3.05 m (10 ft) was the height of the rail on the overhead running track.

The First Rules

THERE WERE 13 rules that Naismith first laid down for his new game:

1. The ball [a standard soccer ball] may be thrown in any direction.
2. The ball may be batted in any direction, but not with the fist.
3. No running with the ball.
4. The ball must be held in the hands, not with any other part of the body.
5. No shouldering, holding, pushing, tripping or striking. The second foul by a player leads to disqualification until next goal.
6. A foul is as indicated in rules 3, 4 and 5.
7. Three consecutive fouls, without any fouls by the opposition will count as a goal against.
8. A goal is scored when the ball is thrown into the basket and stays there.

The original rules stated that the ball must be held only in the hands.

In the first rules, the ball had to stay in the basket for a goal to be scored.

9. If the ball goes out of bounds it will be thrown in by the first person to touch it. This must be done within five seconds; delays count as a foul.

10. The umpire shall be the judge of the men, with the right to disqualify men, as laid out in rule 5.

11. The umpire shall be the judge of the ball, deciding when the ball is in play, out of bounds or when a goal has been scored.

12. The game is two 15-minute halves with a five-minute rest between.

13. The side scoring most goals wins; in the event of a draw the game can continue, with the agreement of the captains, until one side wins.

Early Games

The first game between the men of the Springfield YMCA was a success, although it is recalled that the score was just 1-0. Within weeks, the gallery of the gym was full, with 200 people watching the daily games.

THE FIRST public game of basketball was played between the students and teachers at the Springfield School for Christian Workers; the students won 5-1. When James Naismith invented the indoor game of basketball he did so very much in line with the concepts of Muscular Christianity. It did not take long, however, before the game out-grew its humble origins, even if those origins are remembered to this day.

EARLY RULE CHANGES

NAISMITH HAD ENVISAGED A game with minimal physical contact, but it became clear early on that those playing the game could turn it into a very robust contest indeed. In his original set of rules, Naismith made no indication of the number of players allowed to take part, and in his first article written on the subject in the YMCA's publication, *The Triangle*, he stated that the numbers could be anything between three and 40 per team, depending on the size of

the playing area. Even then he recognised that the greater the number of players, the rougher the game would be.

Alterations to the rules and the way the game was played came along rapidly as the fledgling sport outgrew its Christian origins. By 1896, the game had produced its first professional team and although Naismith was still involved, by 1897 the game had undergone some dramatic changes.

Indoor basketball has been popular with young people since its conception.

Modernisation of the Game

Early changes saw the peach basket replaced by net and the soccer ball replaced by a purpose-designed basketball in 1894. The following year backboards were added to the nets, not so much to allow players to bank the ball, but rather to stop spectators interfering with it on its flight to the net by throwing things.

B Y 1895, FIELD GOALS were worth two points and dribbling had been made legal, although two-handed dribbling was still frowned upon. The same year also saw the introduction of free throws (see p. 220) – an idea that Naismith had originally rejected on the grounds that it would be too easy for an accomplished player to complete.

Although an exhibition event at the 1904 St Louis Olympics, basketball

Proper nets were introduced just a few years after the game was invented.

did not achieve full Olympic status until the Berlin Olympics in 1936. This followed the formation of the International Amateur Basketball Federation (*Federation Internationale de Basketball* – FIBA) in 1932. When it was formed, the FIBA had seven member countries; today it has over 200 members and is one of the most powerful sports governing bodies in existence.

After the Second World War, the popularity of basketball as a sport began to increase worldwide and the first World Basketball Championships were held in 1950.

Perhaps one of the most important decisions to affect basketball, however, was made in 1989, when the FIBA dropped the distinction between amateur and professional players. This move led to the appearance of the American Dream Team at the 1992 Barcelona Olympics, where they took the gold medal and showed the world just what a beautiful game basketball could be.

The memory of those Olympics and the worldwide fascination with everything to do with NBA matches and its stars, has seen basketball grow into one of the biggest sports in the world.

The original soccer ball was exchanged for a specially designed ball in 1894.

The Game in Great Britain

Basketball took a long time to take off in Britain. In the early days it was played only by ex-patriate Americans – mostly in YMCAs – and those who came into direct contact with them. Further additions were made to the playing numbers by students, but by and large the game remained fairly stagnant until the early 1970s.

THE POPULARITY OF the sport until recently was generally low and in the 1960s, the only games that were televised were those played at the Olympics or by the touring team, the Harlem Globetrotters, which were really used to fill a space in the light entertainment schedules.

There had been early attempts to expand the game in Great Britain, but they met with

A game between Czechoslovakia and Italy at the 1960 Rome Olympics.

little success. The Amateur Basketball Association (ABBA) was formed in 1936. The use of two 'B's in the organisation's initials was to avoid confusion with the Amateur Boxing Association (ABA).

The same year that the ABBA was established saw the first national championship. The final, played in Birmingham, was won by Hoylake YMCA and for many years the final was won mostly by teams connected with either the YMCA or with one of the universities.

The Harlem Globetrotters dominated early televised basketball events.

Origins of the Budweiser League

There were attempts to set up a league in 1939, but this collapsed after just a few months. Another attempt was made in 1960, but the organisers failed to persuade the existing London-based sides to join, causing the new league to lack credibility. It staggered on until 1972, when a new league was established that would finally improve the status of basketball in Britain. This competition is now the very successful Budweiser League.

THE IMPACT MADE BY American imports such as Alton Byrd on British basketball certainly helped to capture the

London Towers players celebrate their win in the 1996 Budweiser League.

spectator's imagination and build an understanding of the finer points of the game. Byrd proved to be not only a great player but also an excellent ambassador for the sport.

As in many countries around the world, basketball is now thriving in Britain, and the Budweiser League appears to go from strength to strength. The signing of a number of NBA stars to play in Britain has helped keep the enthusiasm alive. Basketball is now *the* sport for many young Britons, as they try to emulate the heroes of the NBA.

Ongoing initiatives by the English Basketball Association to encourage more young people to play basketball can only be good for a sport that, even in Britain, is beginning to rival soccer in popularity at some schools.

Alton Byrd, who moved from the US to Britain.

The Game in North America

Basketball's development in the US faltered for a
few years after the establishment of the first
professional league in 1898. This was grandly called
the National Basketball League, despite having only
six franchises, all located within a 70-mile radius of
Philadelphia. It also suffered from other leagues
being quickly set up, contesting for players and
audiences within the same geographical area.

THE NATIONAL Basketball League eventually collapsed
in 1903, but there continued to be professional basketball
leagues in America right up to the start of the First World War.
After the war, basketball took another giant step forward, with
the advent of its first truly great side, the Original Celtics. The
team had been formed prior to the war, but came to promin-
ence during the golden sporting age of the 1920s. They played
league basketball and travelled widely to make themselves
known (a practice called 'barnstorming'), grabbing headlines in
the national sporting press like no other team had before.

The Celtics were based in New York but they travelled far
more extensively than any previous basketball side. As a team
that based their play on speed and consistency of line-up they
were a big draw. A steady rise through the 1920s saw the Celtics
decline an offer to join the American Basketball League on the
basis that they could earn more money barnstorming.

The quality of their play was never in doubt. In 1924, over
10,000 people turned up at Madison Square Garden to see
them beat Washington Palace 35-31.

The following year, 1925, the Celts did join the American Basketball League (ABL), winning two straight championships before making a return to barnstorming.

The Boston Celtics evolved from the Original Celtics, based in New York.

Famous Teams

With various basketball leagues throughout North America having a variety of problems – both financial and logisitical – the game continued to grow in the 1920s and 1930s without a real framework for the professional game. The high-school game continued to hold interest, but the real newsmakers of the era were the barnstorming sides. As the Original Celtics fell from grace, their place under the spotlight was taken by the New York Renaissance.

THE NEW YORK RENAISSANCE

UNLIKE THE CELTICS, the Rens toured as a matter of necessity rather than preference. As an all-black side they were barred from the leagues that existed at the time. To ensure that they earned enough money they were often forced to play every day of the week, twice on Saturdays. Although the Rens players faced great hostility in acquiring accommodation on their travels they were always welcomed in the basketball gyms around the country. As a top-quality side they held enormous crowd-pulling potential, which meant a good pay-day for their opponents.

The Renaissance were permitted to play in the World Tournaments that were established as an end-of-season event, and in 1939 they crowned their decade of supremacy by winning the tournament.

The Rens underwent a series of identity changes before disbanding in 1949. By that time they had amassed a total of 2,318 victories with just 318 defeats in 26 seasons of basketball.

THE HARLEM GLOBETROTTERS

ANOTHER ALL-BLACK side that made an indelible imprint on the development of basketball was the Harlem Globetrotters. The Globetrotters started out as a straight basketball team that had to travel, like the Rens, out of necessity. Over a period of 10 years they became so successful that elements of trickery and showmanship were introduced to their game to relieve the boredom of regularly playing inferior sides.

By the 1940s, the Globetrotters were attracting intrigued fans who wanted to see the performance of tricks as much as the basketball. Even then, however, the side were a very accomplished basketball team. In 1940 they won the World Tournament, and although they never repeated the accomplishment, they did beat the World Champions, Minneapolis Lakers, in two exhibition games just after the Second World War.

By a trick of history, the Harlem Globetrotters, as a black basketball team, never achieved the professional acclaim that their standard of

Michael Douglas of the immensely popular Globetrotters.

play deserved. Nevertheless, they did become the most famous and most travelled of all sides. By becoming genuine globe-trotters, they visited more countries than any other basketball team, spreading the game around the world, promoting Naismith's invention wherever they could. In 1951, an all-time record of 75,000 people turned out to see them play an exhibition game in Berlin, Germany.

While the Rens and the Globetrotters were making professional basketball a major attraction, the college basketball scene was also growing. Crowds of up to 10,000 were not uncommon for college games, and players who did not wish to turn professional on leaving college continued to play ball under the auspices of the Amateur Athletic Union.

The early Globetrotters team was responsible for spreading the popularity of basketball worldwide.

Founding of the National Basketball Association

With improved communications and transport systems as well as an improved economy, the development of a unified professional basketball association after the Second World War was inevitable. The National Basketball Association was the result of a merger between two already existing leagues and, although the new organisation had teething problems, under the shrewd leadership of its first Commissioner, Maurice Podoloff, the NBA outlived its early problems.

T HE COLLEGE game also made big strides from 1939, when the National Collegiate Athletic Association (NCAA) agreed to sponsor national invitational championships, the first winners being Oregon. The importance of college and high-school basketball cannot be underestimated. When added together, basketball attracts more fans

The NBA logo on basketball socks.

in the US than baseball and American football combined. In fact, during the period immediately after the Second World War, even after the establishment of the Basketball Association of America (later the National Basketball Association), college basketball continued to be more popular than the professional game. It was felt that college basketball did not rely on the size of players as much as the professional game and as a result was a 'cleaner, crisper' game to watch; a game that had more skill and less physical intensity.

Evidence of basketball's popularity in the US.

The College Game

S UPPORT FOR THE college game first took a dive in 1950 when a series of point-shaving scandals came to light. Players involved would take bribes, not to throw a game but to keep the scores close, for spread-betting purposes. Those caught pointed out that they were young, naive, short of money and that they had not affected the result. Nevertheless, the accusations did much harm to the college game. As soon as there was a hint of such activity in the NBA, players were banned for life. One player pleaded guilty to point-shaving while previously playing amateur basketball. His mitigations were not taken into account and at the age of just 22, his NBA career was immediately halted.

The NBA took its development as a spectator sport very seriously.

University of Florida vs. Louisiana State University.

Having capitalised on the misfortunes of college basketball, the NBA authorities acted to rid the game of its biggest problem: professional time wasting. The most far-reaching change in rules came after two incidents that could have killed off basketball as a spectator sport.

In late 1950, the lowest-ever score was recorded in the NBA when Fort Wayne beat Minneapolis 19-18 due to the fact they used the stalling tactic of simply holding on to the ball for long periods. Just a few weeks later, a game between Rochester and Indianapolis went through six over-times, as each team tried to hold on to the ball, making a no-lose shooting attempt right on the buzzer. In 1954, the 24-second shot-clock was introduced, ruling that a team had to take a shot at goal within 24 seconds of gaining possession of the ball, ensuring the game was played in the spirit of offence.

Modern college basketball.

Timing Changes

THE INTRODUCTION OF the shot-clock and the limiting of team fouls to seven per quarter – those thereafter being penalised with free throws – meant that games would have to be played with an eye to aggressive, attacking ball-play. Such developments, built on the experience of the pioneering players of the 1920s and 1930s, ensured that

basketball would continue to progress and grow as an international sport. The game had already become an Olympic sport, exhibitioning in 1904 at St Louis and becoming a full Olympic sport in Berlin in 1936. Incidentally, on both these occasions the game was played outside, with the Berlin match taking place on a mud and sand pitch that deteriorated considerably during the final – a victory for the US over Canada by the margin of 19-8.

Dennis Rodman demonstrates a jump shot.

BASKETBALL REACHES NEW HEIGHTS

THERE FOLLOWED a time of rapid advancement in the playing of the professional game. Some of the records set in the early days of the NBA are still valid now, but more than that, the game developed as an athletic achievement: jump shots, hook shots, slams and lay-ups all became part of a player's armoury, whereas before, the staple shot had been a straightforward two-handed shot. Dunks had previously been confined to crowd-pleasing warm-up exercises. The athletic grace of basketball players became something that was admired by sports enthusiasts of all persuasions.

Michael Jordan of the Chicago Bulls.

Basketball – A World Sport

B Y THE TIME of the famous 1972 Munich Olympics –
when the USSR beat America on the final buzzer, inflicting
the USA's first-ever Olympic defeat – the game had become
something of an obsession for Americans. It was also now a
truly world sport: an international federation had been
established in 1932 and the game had pulling power across
southern and eastern Europe. Yet despite the growth of the game all over the world, the NBA remains the place where youngsters of all nationalities dream of plying their trade. The college system in America turns out thousands of hopefuls every year, very few of whom actually make it on to an NBA roster.

*Julius Erving
of Philadelphia in
the NBA.*

Legendary Chicago Bulls coach, Phil Jackson.

THE CBA

FOR THOSE WHO refuse to allow the dream to die, the Continental Basketball Association (CBA) acts as a feeder league for the NBA – even Phil Jackson, the now legendary coach who led the Chicago Bulls through their most successful period ever, was once a CBA coach. The CBA was established in 1945 and officially became a Development League for the NBA 40 years later. It claims an impressive array of players who have made the NBA grade after failing to make the draft on leaving college.

Traditionally, those who have failed to make the NBA and have not wished to play in the less financially well-endowed CBA have travelled to other countries.

American Players

American basketball players remain in high demand across the globe, but in recent years the pressure on them to succeed, due to competition from overseas players and increased interest in the sport, has become greater both at home and abroad.

I T IS NOT ONLY youngsters who go to America for sports scholarships, with the intention of playing professional

basketball; adult players from around the globe are also seeking to break into the toughest club league in the world. In 1995, the German Detief Schrempf became the first European to get a place in the All-Star games while he was on the roster with Seattle. The Chicago Bulls' Croatian forward Toni Kukoc was also a well-established player before making the big time with the NBA.

Toni Kukoc, who joined the NBA in 1993.

Many European teams now have American players, boosting the popularity of the sport abroad.

Via television, the impact of the NBA on world basketball is truly amazing. While giving generous support to established basketball organisations across the world, the NBA is also looking to expand its franchising as the demand for top-quality basketball continues to grow. In 1996, Commissioner David Stern indicated the NBA's intentions to expand, not only to incorporate a record number of 32 teams, but also to broaden the geographical scope to include Mexico City and further franchises in Canada.

The movement of American players in the other direction has also been a great help to the development of basketball in countries where the sport has struggled to put down roots. Having access to talented players on a regular basis is another way of furthering the development of the game outside the US, and with an increased awareness of the need for youth coaches and facilities, the game will continue to develop with the help of American ex-patriates.

The Modern Game

One of America's greatest basketball exports was Alton Byrd from San Francisco. Byrd's impact on the British game in the 1980s was immense: he not only played successfully in England and Scotland, picking up a room full of trophies, but he also proved to be a great ambassador for the game. He went on to coach Crystal Palace back into the Premier League after years of second-flight basketball for the south London club.

THE GAME OF BASKETBALL is now at an all-time high. The stadia that NBA teams play in are modern, well-equipped establishments – a far cry from the halls that the pioneers used, which often had posts supporting the building in the middle of the court. At the highest level, coaching and fitness standards are nothing short of supreme, and the game is enjoyed by more and more people every year.

Modern stadia are high-tech and well equipped.

The role of television in the recent development of the game has been crucial. Michael Jordan's abilities could be seen not just by the 20,000 people that attended the Chicago Bulls' games regularly, but also by fans around the world. Packed stadia give a truly exciting atmosphere that those watching at home can tap into. Merchandising helps people still further into the dream and all the time the money generated by television helps underpin further developments across the board.

Television has made global stars of players such as Michael Jordan.

Basketball Today

WHEN JAMES NAISMITH invented basketball as a non-contact sport, one that could be played by any number of players depending on the arena available, he could not have envisaged its development. His vision was of a game that could be played by anybody, not just over-tall people. Today that may seem an oddity when looking at the statistics of players who make up the team rosters of the NBA, but the truth is that Naismith's vision of basketball as a graceful, passing game still holds validity.

In 1996, when the NBA celebrated its 50th anniversary, it noted some interesting comparisons with its opening season. Although the average height of an NBA player was 2.03 m (6 ft 8 in) instead of 1.95 m (6 ft 5 in), the

Former US player Alton Byrd.

smallest player in the league was 1.6 m (5 ft 3 in), while in 1946 the smallest player had been 1.7 m (5 ft 7 in).

The real jump in figures, however, was in the number of those watching the final game. In the 1946–47 season, 7,918 people attended the final, while the 1995–96 final was watched by 24,544 people live and by countless millions around the world on television.

Dennis Rodman during the 1998 NBA finals.

The Game in Australia

The first recorded basketball match to be played in Australia was in 1905 and was played at the Melbourne YMCA. The sport flourished in YMCAs in New South Wales and Victoria and also in church halls, particularly Presbyterian and Anglican.

IN 1931 THE Victoria Basketball Association (VBA) was formed and nine years later the New South Wales Basketball Association was constituted. After the Second World War, associations were formed in the remaining states – South Australia, Queensland, Western Australia and Tasmania. Although it was set up in 1939, the Amateur Basketball Union of Australia – later to be known as the Australian Basketball Federation – did not become fully effective until 1946, when the first Australian championships were held.

In 1949, Australia became an affiliated member of the International Amateur Basketball Federation – the 52nd country to join the world governing body. The 1956 Melbourne Olympics gave basketball a tremendous impetus throughout Australia, and the 1960s saw the emergence of a number of world-class players such as Lindsay Gaze, John Raschke and Ken Cole. The shooting prowess of the great Eddi Palubinskas at the 1972 Munich and 1976 Montreal Olympics mesmerised both spectators and opponents. In more recent years Ian Davies and Andrew Gaze have been leading players.

Basketball is now reckoned to be Australia's fourth most popular sport, and with the 2000 Sydney Olympics on the horizon, the game can look for more extensive exposure. Indeed, there are a number of initiatives to promote basketball in Australia under the Team Basketball Australia banner. The objectives are to develop the sport at all levels, but in particular to produce an Australian international team good enough to challenge for an Olympic medal in the year 2000.

Ricky Grace of the Perth Wildcats.

The Game in Europe

Europe seems to be divided into two camps with regard to basketball. Although the game is not very popular in north-west Europe, in the south and east it has a great following.

BASKETBALL WAS introduced into eastern Europe by YMCA directors who travelled to that part of the world immediately after the First World War. They established the game in cities such as Prague, Budapest and Vienna. Since then the game has also spread to countries such as Spain and Italy, where it now has a large following. In Italy, many basketball teams have links with football clubs and the sport is second in popularity only to soccer. In Britain, Sir John Hall's vision of a sporting club, linking the Newcastle United soccer team with basketball and other sports is based on the way things are done in Italy.

Alessandro Abbio of Bologna.

THE EUROLEAGUE

THE STRONGEST basketball team in Europe is currently Yugoslavia, although the Russians also have a strong side. The Yugoslav national basketball team remained intact during the civil war to claim the World Basketball Championship in 1998. It was their third success in four finals – an impressive record for a nation that was ranked second to last in 1949.

Competition between European clubs began in 1958: the first winners of the Champions' Cup were ASK Riga and the final was contested in front of a crowd of 15,000. Since then the format has changed several times and is now known as the Euroleague. Attendances at these games are growing at an incredible rate (a 338 per cent increase since 1989–90). There are two other major European competitions: the European Cup and the Korac Cup.

ADRIATIC NATIONS

GREECE AND Turkey have strong, well-supported domestic leagues, with successful national set-ups. These countries send their club sides into European competitions with enormous success. In 1997 the Euroleague was won by Olympiakos Pireus, while the Korac Cup was won by Aris Thessalonili, both from Greece.

Evgeni Kisurin of Russia.

The Game in the Rest of the World

While already strongly entrenched in some countries, basketball continues to grow on a global scale. Venezuela, for example, has a league and the number of nations represented in the NBA shows that the game's popularity is still spreading: Australia, Nigeria, Mexico, Lebanon and Zaire all have players in the NBA.

SOUTH AMERICA

DURING AND AFTER the Second World War, basketball was introduced all over the globe by American servicemen. It quickly gained popularity in many countries and, by 1950, the game had caught on so well that the first world championships were being held. The inaugural national World Basketball Championships saw Argentina win the competition. Although the international game became dominated by eastern European teams over the years, Argentina is now making a huge comeback in the international arena.

After Argentina's first success, Brazil won the World Championship on three consecutive occasions. Like Argentina and other South American countries such as Chile, Brazil has a strong domestic basketball scene, with an average of 2,000 people regularly attending the games.

Brazil vs. Puerto Rico in the 1996 Olympics.

CHINA

AS IN MOST SPORTS, the Chinese are considered to have massive potential to take on the best at basketball. The game is easy and cheap to set up, and therefore lends itself to a nation strong in personnel, but weaker than other countries financially. The Chinese have already won the Asian Games basketball title and have not yet reached the top of their game.

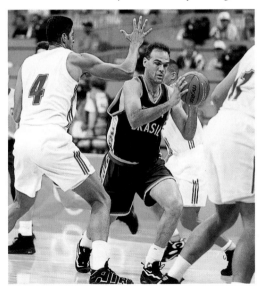

English Basketball Association

It was only after the English Basketball Association (EBBA) – the successor to the Amateur Basketball Association – introduced a number initiatives in the 1970s that the sport really began to develop.

I T WAS THE energy and vision of the EBBA's first full-time administrator, Mel Welch, that helped transform basketball from what it was – very much a minority sport – to the multi-million pound game it is today.

The EBBA is now at the fore-front of organising basketball at all levels. There is a pyramid system in operation for men's, women's and youth basketball and the game is also being

John Insall, one of the stars of basketball's early days of popularity in England.

promoted in schools in a way that has never been done before.

The EBBA is recognised as one of the more progressive sports governing bodies and continues to oversee the expansion of the game throughout the country. The EBBA produces a range of publications, including manuals on coaching and officiating, wallcharts and pamphlets on the game. It is also responsible for coaching and refereeing qualifications. In addition, the organisation can provide information on training camps and clinics.

The EBBA organises games at all levels, including youth level.

Women's Basketball

It took women just two years from the game's invention to get in on the basketball act. The first game played by women was held in Northampton, Massachusetts, in 1893. No men were allowed in the hall and there is a story that peeping toms had to be shooed away from the windows.

DESPITE TAKING the game up at an early stage, women had to wait a long time before their participation was taken seriously. In England, the game of netball was developed from basketball as a more genteel game for women and girls to play. Even in America, a strange seven-a-side game was developed.

WOMEN'S CHAMPIONSHIPS

WOMEN STARTED TO play the full game across the world long before women's basketball was properly established in America. In 1965, an English women's championship was established, but in America,

An English championship for women was established in 1965.

women's basketball only came to the fore in preparation for the 1976 Olympics – the first time women's basketball became an Olympic sport. Lagging behind the rest of the world, they failed to make an impact.

There is now, however, a strong women's basketball scene in America. Not only is there a women's NBA, fully affiliated to the men's game, but there is also a flourishing college set-up. The Women's National Basketball Association (WNBA) sides are professional outfits, sponsored by the male NBA sides. They play in NBA arenas on full-size courts, with the same rules. The most successful team is the Houston Comets, who have emulated their male counterparts by winning back-to-back Championships in 1996–97 and 1997–98.

In 1985, Lynette Woodward joined the Harlem Globetrotters, becoming the first female professional to play against men.

Women's basketball: Sheffield vs. Birmingham.

Sponsorship

The American Dream Team that won the 1992 Olympic Games in Barcelona, and the resulting adulation of players such as Michael Jordan, Larry Bird and 'Magic' Johnson, raised the profile of basketball to unforeseen heights. There was the sudden belief that basketball could go on to become the most popular team sport in the world.

The NBA became the key brand in the sport, attracting sponsorship from many large companies.

THE KEY BRAND was the NBA. It seemed every potential sponsor – and indeed broadcaster – in the world wanted to be associated with the top professional American stars and started to invest vast sums of money in any activity that involved the NBA or carried its logo.

At the height of his earning powers, Michael Jordan was said to have earned $35 million in 1995 on endorsements alone, making him the highest-paid sportsman in the land. The same year he also pulled in about $4 million as a basketball player.

Leading sports clothing companies vied for licensing rights to the NBA's clothing and apparel business, which has developed into a huge operation not only in the United States but also throughout the rest of the world.

Basketball is now big business. It is not only the likes of adidas, Nike and Reebok who are anxious to be associated with the thriving game of basketball; the restaurant chain McDonalds and brewers Budweiser are just two large commercial organisations who have signed long-term deals to have their brands linked to the sport, and many others are following suit.

Sports companies vie for sponsorship of the big teams and names.

COMPETITIONS
US Competitions

> Although basketball was invented in the United States in 1891, it was not until 1946 that a truly national league was formed – the Basketball Association of America, the forerunner of the National Basketball Association.

BEFORE THIS THERE were several attempts to start leagues containing teams spread over a wide geographical areas, but because of a number problems – mainly financial – they all failed.

A series of so-called World Tournaments were held between the wars but interest was more in individual clubs playing exhibition games than organised league encounters.

NCCA IS ESTABLISHED

IN THE 1920s and 1930s college basketball was far more popular than the professional leagues (barnstorming

College basketball competitions remain very popular.

was also still popular) and their competitions attracted a great deal of interest from the American public. Since 1938, the National Collegiate Athletic Association (NCAA) has organised the National College Championship, which still receives widespread television coverage. The NCAA governs the game in over 500 American colleges and universities.

THE NBA IS FORMED

SINCE THE FORMATION of the NBA the status of the game has changed dramatically and the professional game is the one that has caught the imagination of public and broadcasters alike.

The introduction of variations of the game of basketball, such as the All-Star games, which are annual events designed to showcase an individual's talents, have also increased in popularity. Individual and team showdowns involving shooting skills are also highly popular, and, it must be said, very competitive.

Clyde Drexler for the West in the NBA All-Star.

The National Basketball Association

The National Basketball Association (NBA) was established when the National Basketball League (NBL) merged with the Basketball Association of America (BAA). Prior to the NBA's formation, a number of attempts had been made to run professional and semi-professional basketball leagues, all with little success.

BAA'S FORMATION

THE BASKETBALL Association of America, formed in 1946 was, in effect, the beginning of the NBA. The new organisation saw the need to play regular professional basketball in metropolitan areas, bringing in advertising, television and large crowds to compete with baseball and ice hockey as a major spectator sport. All the new clubs were affiliated to a major city, rather than a company, as had been the case with many NBL sides, and all played out of proper venues instead of school halls.

Over 7,000 fans turned up for the first game, a match-up between Toronto and New York, held on 1 November 1946. For that season, the schedule was a 60-game fixture list. Today 82 games are played, excluding play-offs.

The NBL and BAA formally merged to create the NBA on 3 August 1949. While the BAA had brought with it a sounder structure and organised fixture lists, the NBL was the organisation that had the registration of the best-known players who would pull in the crowds.

The formation of the NBA enabled basketball to compete with baseball and ice hockey as a popular spectator sport.

PODOLOFF AND THE NBA

THE ASSOCIATION'S first Commissioner was Maurice Podoloff, a small man with a big vision. It was Podoloff who ensured that the new organisation was put on a sound footing, organising the NBA's early live television coverage. It was also Podoloff who capitalised on the scandals that were connected with college basketball, using them to promote the NBA as a clean organisation, free from such scandal.

Several stories had emerged about gambling and point-shaving in college basketball, which had alienated many supporters.

When there was any question of such activities within the NBA, Podoloff acted quickly to expel for life any players that may have been implicated – proof of involvement was not

necessarily needed to end a player's career. Since those days of strict behaviour, the NBA has become America's top sporting organisation.

THE NBA TODAY

THE STADIA that NBA sides play in are regularly oversubscribed, with enormous television deals ensuring that millions across the world are able to watch the games.

One of the most famous sportsmen in the world, Michael Jordan, is a product of the NBA, and certainly some of the best paid sports stars are the supreme athletes that compete in the National Basketball Association.

NBA players are the best-paid stars in the sport.

Past Winners

THE FIRST LEAGUE winners of the BAA in 1946–47 were the Washington Capitols in the Eastern Division and the Chicago Stags in the Western Division. Philadelphia won the inter-divisional play-offs, defeating Chicago four games to one to become the first champions. For the first formal year of the NBA the divisional winners were the Syracuse Nationals, the Minneapolis Lakers and the Indianapolis Olympians. The Lakers eventually won the play-off final against Syracuse.

The most successful NBA side of all time is unquestionably the Boston Celtics. The Celtics first won the Championship in 1956–57 and over the next 14 years they won the Championship another 10 times. In addition to the Championship, they were also divisional winners on no less than 13 occasions over the same period. Since then, Boston have won the Championship on a further five occasions, winning their divisional Conference seven times.

Larry Bird of the Boston Celtics, the most successful NBA team of all time.

Jerry Reinsdorf (centre), owner of the Chicago Bulls, who won the Championship three years running in 1995–98.

The most successful Western Conference side has been Los Angeles. LA won their first Conference in 1960–61, repeating the feat the following year. In all they have won their league 18 times, but have only gone on to win the Championship on six occasions.

The most successful team in recent years has been the Chicago Bulls. The Bulls did not win their Conference play-offs until 1990–91, but they then became the team of the decade by winning the Championship three years running. They failed to make the final in 1993–94 and again in 1994–95, but they then resumed their position as champions for the next three seasons until San Antonio broke their winning streak in 1999.

NBA CHAMPIONS

1946–47	Philadelphia Warriors	1969–70	New York Knicks
1947–48	Baltimore Bullets	1970–71	Milwaukee Bucks
1948–49	Minneapolis Lakers	1971–72	Los Angeles Lakers
1949–50	Minneapolis Lakers	1972–73	New York Knicks
		1973–74	Boston Celtics
1950–51	Rochester Royals	1974–75	Golden State Warriors
1951–52	Minneapolis Lakers		
1952–53	Minneapolis Lakers	1975–76	Boston Celtics
1953–54	Minneapolis Lakers	1976–77	Portland Trail Blazers
1954–55	Syracuse Nationals		
1955–56	Philadelphia Warriors		
1956–57	Boston Celtics		
1957–58	St Louis Hawks		
1958–59	Boston Celtics		
1959–60	Boston Celtics		
1960–61	Boston Celtics		
1961–62	Boston Celtics		
1962–63	Boston Celtics		
1963–64	Boston Celtics		
1964–65	Boston Celtics		
1965–66	Boston Celtics		
1966–67	Philadelphia 76ers		
1967–68	Boston Celtics		
1968–69	Boston Celtics		

Clyde Drexler of the 1994–95 Champions, Houston Rockets.

1977–78	Washington Bullets	1990–91	Chicago Bulls
1978–79	Seattle SuperSonics	1991–92	Chicago Bulls
1979–80	Los Angeles Lakers	1992–93	Chicago Bulls
1980–81	Boston Celtics	1993–94	Houston Rockets
1981–82	Los Angeles Lakers	1994–95	Houston Rockets
1982–83	Philadelphia 76ers	1995–96	Chicago Bulls
1983–84	Boston Celtics	1996–97	Chicago Bulls
1984–85	Los Angeles Lakers	1997–98	Chicago Bulls
1985–86	Boston Celtics	1998–99	San Antonio Spurs
1986–87	Los Angeles Lakers		
1987–88	Los Angeles Lakers		
1988–89	Detroit Pistons		
1989–90	Detroit Pistons		

Chicago Bulls players celebrate their 1998 NBA win.

NBA All-Star Games

It was back in 1951 that NBA public relations
director Haskell Cohen, sitting in his office on
the 80th floor of the Empire State Building,
came up with a proposal for the creation of an
All-Star game. The plan involved a match
between the pick of the players from the Eastern
and Western Conferences.

THERE WAS MUCH scepticism amongst Cohen's fellow
officials, who felt that such a competition would not attract
enough public interest. However, Cohen received the support of
Boston owner Walter Brown, who fully endorsed the idea and
predicted the planned match would rival that of the successful
baseball All-Star game. Brown was so confident that Cohen's
plan would be a public relations and commercial success that he
offered Boston Garden as a free venue for the event.

On 2 March 1951,
the NBA staged its first
All-Star game before a
crowd of 10,094. The
Eastern Conference, who
had brilliant offensive
players such as Ed
Macauley, Joe Fulks and
Dolph Schayes in their

*An East-West All-Star game
in 1996.*

starting line-up, strolled to a comfortable 111–94 win over the George Mikan-led Western Conference. The game was a great success and did indeed provide a showcase for the skills and talents of the NBA players, opening up a whole new audience for the sport. The All-Star game attracted the interest of the television companies and boosted the image of basketball: the combined efforts of Cohen and Brown were well rewarded.

For the next 30 years or so, the All-Star game continued to be a high-profile and successful mid-season break from the regular-season grind. It continued to attract the support of the great players of the period, including Wilt Chamberlain, Oscar Robertson and Bob Pettit. However, the early 1980s saw an incredible boost in the popularity of the NBA and the All-Star game started to develop into the four-day extravaganza that it is today.

Wilt Chamberlain in 1976.

Past Winners

EAST-WEST ALL-STAR GAMES

1951	East 111	West 94	1978	East 133	West 125
1952	East 108	West 91	1979	West 134	East 129
1953	West 79	East 75	1980	East 144	West 136*
1954	East 98	West 93*	1981	East 123	West 120
1955	East 100	West 91	1982	East 120	West 118
1956	West 108	East 94	1983	East 132	West 123*
1957	East 109	West 97	1984	East 154	West 145*
1958	East 130	West 118	1985	West 140	East 129
1959	West 124	East 108	1986	East 139	West 132
1960	East 125	West 115	1987	West 154	East 149*
1961	West 153	East 131	1988	East 138	West 133
1962	West 150	East 130	1989	West 143	East 134
1963	East 115	West 108	1990	East 130	West 113
1964	East 111	West 107	1991	East 116	West 114
1965	East 124	West 124	1992	West 153	East 113
1966	East 137	West 94	1993	West 135	East 132*
1967	West 135	East 120	1994	East 127	West 118
1968	East 144	West 124	1995	West 139	East 112
1969	East 123	West 112	1996	East 129	West 118
1970	East 142	West 135	1997	East 132	West 120
1971	West 108	East 107	1998	East 135	West 114
1972	West 112	East 110	1999	Not held because of
1973	East 104	West 84		players' dispute
1974	West 134	East 123		
1975	East 108	West 102	* Game went into overtime
1976	East 123	West 109		
1977	West 125	East 124		

Clyde Drexler playing for the West in the 1996 NBA All-Star game.

NBA Slam Dunk Championship/ Long Distance Three-Point Shooting Contest

IN 1984, THE All-Star Saturday was introduced as a taster for the public to the All-Star game that had traditionally been played on Sundays. The first All-Star Saturday included a whole range of events designed to entertain and whet the appetite of both the fans and the media. However, it was the Slam Dunk Championship, featuring individual competitors, that best caught the public's imagination, with Phoenix forward Larry Nance winning the inaugural event. Michael Jordan famously won the contest in 1987 and 1988, at a time when both his and basketball's stars were in the ascendancy. The competition ceased in 1997 when the fees commanded by the players could no longer be met.

In 1986, the Long Distance Three-Point Shooting Contest was introduced, and for the first three years was dominated by Boston forward Larry Bird.

Larry Bird of the Boston Celtics.

SLAM DUNK CHAMPIONSHIP

Year	Player	Team
1984	Larry Nance	Phoenix
1985	Dominique Wilkins	Atlanta
1986	Spud Webb	Atlanta
1987	Michael Jordan	Chicago
1988	Michael Jordan	Chicago
1989	Kenny Walker	New York
1990	Dominique Wilkins	Atlanta
1991	Dee Brown	Boston
1992	Cedric Ceballos	Phoenix
1993	Harold Miner	Miami
1994	Isaiah Rider	Minnesota
1995	Harold Miner	Miami
1996	Brent Barry	LA Clippers
1997	Kobe Bryant	LA Lakers

LONG DISTANCE THREE-POINT
SHOOTING CONTEST

Year	Player	Team
1986	Larry Bird	Boston
1987	Larry Bird	Boston
1988	Larry Bird	Boston
1989	Dale Ellis	Seattle
1990	Craig Hodges	Chicago
1991	Craig Hodges	Chicago
1992	Craig Hodges	Chicago
1993	Mark Price	Cleveland
1994	Mark Price	Cleveland
1995	Glen Rice	Miami
1996	Tim Legler	Washington
1997	Steve Kerr	Chicago
1998	Jeff Hornacek	Utah
1999	Not held because of players' dispute	

Long Distance Three-Point champion Larry Bird.

BY 1993, THE All-Star game weekend had been extended to include Thursday and Friday as well. The additional days now include a variety of meet-the-stars sessions, seminars, Jam Session hoop festivals and three-on-three contests.

The All-Star game festival is now an integral part of the basketball season and is designed to offer the basketball-hungry public everything they might desire.

Michael Jordan, Slam Dunk champion 1987–88.

British Competitions

Although a governing body, the Amateur Basketball Association (ABBA), was formed in 1936, British basketball didn't boast any major competitions of note – certainly none that caught the public's interest – until 1972. In that year, a new national league was introduced and the widespread success of the competition was to change the destiny of basketball in Britain.

S ERIOUS CLUB sponsorship was introduced in 1973, after which attendances began to increase rapidly, and from that time the national competition has grown into the success story now called the Budweiser League. There are two more competitions during the season in addition to the popular Budweiser League.

1998 Budweiser League.

THE ENGLISH BASKETBALL ASSOCIATION

THE FIRST BRITISH basketball championship took place in 1936 between two teams that were essentially comprised of American ex-patriates. The game was not established as an indigenous sport until 1972, when the English Basketball Association was established, with six teams.

The fledgling league quickly changed the make-up of British basketball, giving it a framework for professionalism and improvement. The number of clubs also rose rapidly, as did the quality of players, both local talent and those who came across from America to play.

London Towers win the Budweiser League in 1996.

THE BASKETBALL LEAGUE

THE QUALITY OF the game improved to such a degree that Britain's leading team, Crystal Palace, reached the quarter-finals of the European Cup in 1975, a feat they were to repeat in 1981. With increased public interest in the game and a television deal that put British basketball on the small screen for the first time in 1984, the game and its commercial potential grew rapidly.

Briefly, in an attempt to exploit the commercial possibilities, football clubs became involved with running their own basketball teams at that time; the most notable were Manchester United, Portsmouth and Glasgow Rangers. The link-up did not last, however, and the final team to fold was Glasgow Rangers in 1988–89.

In the meantime, the Basketball League was established in 1987 as a Premiership League. In the same way that the Premiership was established in English football, this move was a means of basketball clubs taking on their own sponsorship responsibilities, leaving the EBBA to concentrate on the overall governing of the sport at a national level.

English basketball: the London Leopards vs. the Manchester Giants.

The Budweiser League

SPONSORSHIP

THE BASKETBALL League's first sponsorship deal was with Carlsberg; Budweiser took over in 1992. The second of Budweiser's two three-year deals was worth £2.5 million to the British game and has helped raise the awareness of both the sport and the product over the seven years that the two have been linked together. A third period of sponsorship is now underway. The initial Basketball League had 15 teams in it; the current number challenging for the Championship is 13.

THE LEAGUE TODAY

ALTHOUGH THERE are now two teams less than when the league was first inaugurated, standards of arenas and facilities have improved dramatically, ensuring that at its highest level the game is watched in the appropriate surroundings.

For the encore at the end of the regular season, as in America, a championship play-off takes place. Eight teams play off, but the knock-out competition

Sponsorship has allowed the British game to expand.

brings the number of teams who go to Wembley to four; the top team plays the eighth, the second plays the seventh, and so on. This event has run since the 1978–79 season and is held at Wembley over two days, attracting huge crowds. The Budweiser League is at the pinnacle of British basketball, and while it may be dominated by Americans at the moment, there is no reason why British players cannot work towards matching the standards of their counterparts from the United States.

With a structure that involves the coaching and development of young players and a worthwhile league to aim for, young British basketball players have never been in a better position to make an impact on the professional game.

Birmingham Bullets in the 1997 Budweiser League.

Past Winners

THE FIRST WINNER of the National League established by the EBBA was Avenue, from Leyton, in east London. In the first 15 years of the competition, while it was run by the EBBA, the title was picked up by Crystal Palace on seven occasions. It left London just six times. The End-of-Season

Championship, which was established in 1978, was won by Crystal Palace four times before the competition was taken over by the Basketball League in 1987. The inaugural Basketball League was won by Portsmouth in 1987–88, with Livingston from Scotland being the Champions, beating Portsmouth 81-72 in the final. The following year,

Greater London Leopards vs. Manchester Giants in 1998.

with Portsmouth defunct, Livingston again went to the final, this time losing to the new league title holders, Glasgow.

The most successful team in the history of British basketball was the Crystal Palace side of the 1980s, but since the inception of the Basketball League, Kingston have won the league a record three seasons on the run from 1989–92. In all three of those years they went on to win the Championship. The following year, the Kingston franchise was moved to Guildford, where it remained for just two years before being sold on to east London at the Docklands Arena, taking the name Leopards.

Now the Greater London Leopards side have won the league two years running (1996/97–1997/98), but have picked up the Championship just once. Sheffield have also won the league on two occasions: 1994–95 and 1998–99. No other team has headed the league on more than one occasion, although Worthing Bears, who won the league in 1992–93 won the Championship three years on the trot (1992/93–1994/95).

BUDWEISER LEAGUE WINNERS

1987–88	Portsmouth
1988–89	Glasgow
1989–90	Kingston
1990–91	Kingston
1991–92	Kingston
1992–93	Worthing
1993–94	Thames Valley
1994–95	Sheffield
1995–96	London
1996–97	Greater London
1997–98	Greater London
1998–99	Sheffield

The Greater London Leopards logo, winners of the 1997 and 1998 league.

The Greater London Leopards.

The Uni-Ball Trophy

The Uni-Ball Trophy is the major knock-out trophy for teams that compete in the Basketball League. It was established in 1987–88 and before Uni-Ball took over the sponsorship it was known as the 7-Up Trophy. After their initial sponsorship of one year in 1997–98, Uni-Ball signed a five-year deal worth £1.2 million. It was the longest single sponsorship deal in the history of British basketball.

T HE COMPETITION IS run on a pool basis for the initial stage. In its first year there were four pools, but after running the competition on a two- and three-pool basis, the

The launch of the Uni-Ball Trophy sponsorship.

organisers finally settled on a two-pool system in 1995–96. The competition is currently contested by 13 teams. The previous champions get a bye to the quarter-finals and the remaining teams are divided into North and South pools, playing the other teams in their pool once, with an even number of home and away games. From the pool stages the competition reverts to a knock-out format through the quarter- and semi-finals and culminates in a one-game final.

The venue for the Uni-Ball Trophy final has been Birmingham for all but two years of the competition (it was held at the Albert Hall in London in 1990–91 and 1991–92). At the venue, immediately prior to the final, a coaching clinic is run for 13–17-year-olds. This is the biggest indoor clinic for any sport in the UK and ensures a large turnout of young people for the final itself.

The Sheffield Sharks, Uni-Ball Trophy winners in 1998.

Past Winners

THE UNI-BALL TROPHY'S first-ever winners were
Scottish outfit Livingston. Since its inception 12 years ago,
the trophy has been won by seven different sides. Livingston
returned to the NEC for the second year, but failed to pick up
the trophy, losing to Bracknell 89-81.

The basketball franchise now based in Bracknell is the
Thames Valley Tigers. They first won the trophy in 1992–93,

beating Guildford
91-84. The Tigers
retained the trophy for
the next two years, with
wins over Manchester
(79-73) and Sheffield
(74-69). Those three
consecutive wins makes
Thames Valley the most
successful side in this
tournament.

London Towers
broke the Tigers'
winning streak, when
they took the trophy in
1995–96, with a victory
against Worthing
(90-84).

*Todd Cauthorn
of Sheffield with the
Uni-Ball Trophy.*

The year after, Towers were again victorious, this time against Chester (76-59). However, although they reached the NEC finals for a third consecutive year in 1997–98, Towers failed to overcome the Sheffield Sharks, going down 82-79. Sheffield themselves had been defeated finalists in 1994–95. Manchester managed to reach the finals on three separate occasions, coming away with runners-up medals each time, before they finally took the trophy in 1999.

If name changes and relocations are not taken into account, then Kingston/Guildford could be considered the most successful side in the competition. Kingston took the trophy three years running from 1989–92, beating Manchester twice at the Albert Hall and then Leicester at Birmingham. The following season, 1992–93, Guildford were the beaten finalists as Thames Valley set out on their three-year winning run.

John Amaschi of Sheffield in the 1996 Uni-Ball Trophy final.

UNI-BALL TROPHY WINNERS

1987–88	Livingston
1988–89	Bracknell
1989–90	Kingston
1990–91	Kingston
1991–92	Kingston
1992–93	Thames Valley

1993–94	Thames Valley
1994–95	Thames Valley
1995–96	London Towers
1996–97	London Towers
1997–98	Sheffield
1998–99	Manchester

The winning Sheffield team, 1998.

The All-Star Games

The All-Star games in Britain take place annually in the second half of the season. They were established in 1988–89 and are a showcase for British basketball. The format is based on the American competition, whereby the best players are selected on a regional basis for an annual fixture.

B Y BRINGING together the best players in the British league, the organisers can put on a display of basketball that should encourage all who see the game to either attend games regularly or take up the sport for themselves. The teams are selected on a North/South basis. They were once selected by ballot of the fans, but now the selection is much more scientific, with players' stats being taken into account. Whatever the method of selection, to be picked for the All-Stars game is a highlight in the career of a player in the British Basketball League.

With little at stake, the nature of North/South games is always that they are fast, furious and entertaining. It is an opportunity for players to try out training-session tricks, with slams and other fancy tricks abounding. In one

sense the games are not very competitive, but they are eagerly anticipated by the players as a means of expressing their individual talents on the basketball court. Teamwork and defence are not the watchwords and usually the games are very high-scoring. The event is held at various venues, but a good crowd is always assured, with casual basketball fans appreciating the carnival atmosphere of the event.

Fans of the All-Star game.

Past Winners

THE FIRST All-Star fixture between North and South was played in the 1988–89 season, with the North winning 154-148. The North then won the next two fixtures before the South finally won in 1991–92 by the margin 150-137.

In the 11 years that the games have been held, the North have won five and the South six. The biggest winning margin was achieved in 1996–97 when the North, coached by Nick Nurse, won 162-148. The following year was the highest-scoring game when the South came back to win 173-166.

The only person to be elected Most Valuable Player (MVP) in the All-Star games more than once is John Tresvant. Tresvant gained his awards in 1991–92 and 1992–93. Playing for the North he was on the losing side in the first year (150-137) and the winning side the second year (150-141).

John Tresvant (left), the only All-Star MVP double winner.

Karl Brown (left), who has appeared in six All-Star games.

Three players (Kevin St Kitts, Nigel Lloyd and Karl Brown) have appeared in six All-Star games, but Peter Scantlebury and Russ Saunders are the only two players to have participated in seven games. Both players are long-serving members of the British basketball scene, Scantlebury being English, while Saunders is American.

The only coach to have been selected to run an All-Star team more than twice is Kevin Cadle. He coached All-Star games in the first four years of their existence. In the first season (1988–89) he was the head coach at Glasgow, thus heading up the victorious North side. Thereafter, Cadle was down South and was on the losing side for two years before winning again in 1991–92. Cadle is unquestionably the most successful coach that British basketball has ever had. He has coached the national teams of England, Scotland and Great Britain, and his honours list includes winning the league title five times and the Championship five times.

BRITISH ALL-STAR GAMES WINNERS

1988–89	North 154	South 148
1989–90	North 133	South 125
1990–91	North 139	South 132
1991–92	South 150	North 137
1992–93	North 150	South 141
1993–94	South 148	North 140
1994–95	South 164	North 151
1995–96	South 157	North 153
1996–97	North 162	South 148
1997–98	South 173	North 166
1998–99	South 158	North 156

The National Cup

The National Cup was first established in 1978–79 as a knock-out competition. In 1997–88 the competition was taken over by Premier League teams. The number of sides competing is made up to 16 by the top sides from the previous season's first division.

A S A KNOCK-OUT competition that includes the top sides, the National Cup has always managed to attract sponsorship. Currently it is sponsored by Sainsbury's Classic Cola. This sponsorship is four years old and set to run for at

The Sainsbury's Classic Cola National Cup.

least another year. Previous sponsors have included Coca-Cola and Chrysalis television company. With the Budweiser League currently being 13 teams strong, the first division will provide three sides to compete in the first round of the National Cup.

Games are played on a once-only basis in the first two rounds, with the semi-final being a two-legged event. Prior to 1991–92, the semi-finals had also been a single-game affair.

The final, just one match, is played at a major venue. Over the last four years of the competition the final has been played at Sheffield, even though Sheffield Sharks were finalists on only three of those occasions. Previously the final had been held at the Albert Hall, London Arena, or in Doncaster. No team outside the Premiership has ever reached the final of the competition, although Crystal Palace reached the semi-finals in 1995–96, the year before they entered the Budweiser League.

The 1998 men's national basketball final at the Sheffield Arena.

Past Winners

BEFORE THE formation of the Budweiser League, the National Cup had been won by just four teams over the nine years of its existence. The inaugural competition of 1978–79 was won by Doncaster, with Crystal Palace as the runners-up. Crystal Palace then won the trophy two years running before Solent won it for three years, then Kingston for three years.

Since the formation of the Basketball League, however, no one team has really dominated the competition. The first winners in 1987–88 were Kingston, who beat Portsmouth 90-84. Kingston won the competition again in 1989–90 and 1991–92, with Guildford winning in 1992–93. Bracknell picked up the Cup in 1988–89, Sunderland in 1990–91.

Since then, the competition has been won by a number of different teams: Worthing, Sheffield (twice), London Leopards, and Thames Valley. Both Thames Valley and Sheffield managed to reach the final a further two times in that period, ending as runners-up. Thames Valley are the least successful

The Thames Valley Tigers receive their trophy in 1998.

Dameon Page (left) of the 1998 winning Thames Valley Tigers.

finalists, having failed to lift the trophy on three of their four final appearances.

The most one-sided final took place at the London Arena in 1989–90 when Kingston defeated Sunderland by the margin of 103-78. The closest final was in 1997–98 when Thames Valley vanquished Leicester 82-78. Overall, Kingston/Guildford are the most successful team in the National Cup, having won the competition seven times. The next most successful side remains Solent, who no longer play in the Basketball League.

NATIONAL CUP WINNERS

1987–88	Kingston	1993–94	Worthing
1988–89	Bracknell	1994–95	Sheffield
1989–90	Kingston	1995–96	London
1990–91	Sunderland	1996–97	Greater London
1991–92	Kingston	1997–98	Thames Valley
1992–93	Guildford	1998–99	Sheffield

The International Game

Basketball was introduced as a demonstration sport at the 1904 St Louis Olympic Games, but worldwide interest was limited, as all the teams entered were from the United States. It was next entered as a demonstration sport at the 1924 Paris Olympics and teams from France, Britain, Italy and the United States took part, with the Central London YMCA winning the gold medal.

I N 1932 THE International Amateur Basketball Federation (FIBA) was formed and included seven countries; today FIBA has over 200 member countries. The new international governing body began to lobby immediately for basketball's acceptance as a serious international sport, and in 1936 it was included in the Berlin Olympics as a full competitive event.

After gaining Olympic status, the game quickly spread around the world.

Tzanis Stavrakopoulas of Panathinaikos.

The first World Championships were held in 1950 and were won by Argentina, although eastern Europe has largely dominated international basketball for most of the time since the early 1950s.

Argentina and several other South American countries have strong domestic competitions, as do Israel, Greece, Cyprus and Turkey.

Spain's Liga ACB and Italy's A-1 League are rated as two of the strongest competitions outside the NBA. In fact, the continent of Europe as a whole provides some of the most competitive and exciting basketball leagues in the world.

The first European club competition was started in 1958 and the first winners were ASK Riga. The format of the championship has changed several times since then and is now known as the Euroleague. Teams from Europe also compete for the European Cup and the Korac Cup.

CSKA Moscow vs. Panathinaikos.

Euroleague Past Winners

EUROPEAN CLUB CHAMPIONSHIP

1957–58	ASK Riga – Akademik Sophia 86-81, 71-84
1958–59	ASK Riga – Akademik Sophia 79-58, 67-69
1959–60	ASK Riga – Dynamo Tbilisi 69-62, 61-57
1960–61	CSKA Moscow – ASK Riga 61-66, 87-62
1961–62	Dynamo Tbilisi – Real Madrid 90-83
1962–63	CSKA Moscow – Real Madrid 86-69, 74-91 (99-80)
1963–64	Real Madrid – Spartak Brno 99-110, 84-64
1964–65	Real Madrid – CSKA Moscow 81-88, 76-62
1965–66	Simmenthal Milan – Slavia Praha 77-72
1966–67	Real Madrid – Simmenthal Milan 91-83
1967–68	Real Madrid – Spartak Brno 98-95
1968–69	CSKA Moscow – Real Madrid 103-99
1969–70	Ignis Varese – CSKA Moscow 79-74
1970–71	CSKA Moscow – Ignis Varese 67-53
1971–72	Ignis Varese – Jugoplastika Split 70-69
1972–73	Ignis Varese – CSKA Moscow 71-66
1973–74	Real Madrid – Ignis Varese 84-82
1974–75	Ignis Varese – Real Madrid 79-66
1975–76	Mobilgirgi Varese – Real Madrid 81-74
1976–77	Maccabi Tel-Aviv – Mobilgirgi Varese 78-77
1977–78	Real Madrid – Mobilgirgi Varese 75-67
1978–79	Bosna Sarajevo – Emerson Varese 96-93
1979–80	Real Madrid – Maccabi Tel-Aviv 89-85
1980–81	Maccabi Tel-Aviv – Synudine Bologna 80-79
1981–82	Sqibb Cantu – Maccabi Tel-Aviv 86-80
1982–83	Ford Cantu – Billy Milan 69-68

EUROPEAN CUP

1983–84 Banco di Roma –
Barcelona 79-73
1984–85 Cibona Zagreb –
Real Madrid 87-78
1985–86 Cibona Zagreb –
Zalgiris Kaunas 94-82
1986–87 Tracer Milan –
Maccabi Tel-Aviv 71-69
1987–88 Tracer Milan –
Maccabi Tel-Aviv 90-84
1988–89 Jugoplastika Split –
Maccabi Tel-Aviv 75-69
1989–90 Jugoplastika Split –
FC Barcelona 72-67
1990–91 Pop 84 Split –
Barcelona 70-65

Joe Arlauckas of Real Madrid.

EUROPEAN LEAGUE

1991–92 Partizan Beograd –
Joventut Badalona 71-70
1992–93 Limoges –
Benetton Treviso 59-55
1993–94 Joventut Badalona –
Olympiakos Pireus 59-57
1994–95 Real Madrid – Olympiakos 73-61
1995–96 Panathinaikos Athens – FC Barcelona 67-66

Panagiotis Giannakis of Panathinaikos.

EUROLEAGUE

1996–97 Olympiakos Pireus – FC Barcelona 73-58
1997–98 Kinder Bologna – AEK Athens 58-44

THE PLAYERS
Top 20 Players in the US

KAREEM ABDUL-JABBAR

KAREEM ABDUL-JABBAR had an NBA career that spanned 20 years from 1969 when he was the NBA Rookie of the Year. He appeared in over 1,500 games, scoring a total of 15,837 field goals. He picked up a record six MVPs (Most Valuable Player awards), three each in games for Milwaukee and the LA Lakers. In addition to his scoring ability, Abdul-Jabbar was also a leading defensive player. On one occasion in 1975 he made a total of 29 rebounds in one game against Detroit. Over his 20-year career he blocked no less than 2,189 shots, topping that particular table for the season on four occasions.

Kareem Abdul-Jabbar in his Lakers' days.

After his career in the NBA, Abdul-Jabbar continued to play basketball, joining the world-touring Harlem Globetrotters, bringing basketball as pure entertainment to thousands of people.

'SIR' CHARLES BARKLEY

'SIR' CHARLES BARKLEY was part of the same all-rookie team as Michael Jordan and Hakeem Olajuwon, signing for Philadelphia in 1984. In 1992–93, his first year with Phoenix, he collected an MVP while leading the Suns to the NBA final. During the season he averaged 25.6 points per game and 12.2 blocked shots. He was later traded to Houston.

The outspoken Barkley held the NBA record for taking the most offensive rebounds for three consecutive seasons, starting in 1986–87. His strength inside led to him having one of the best percentage records ever for field shots made. One of the modern games' most consistent players, the powerful Barkley soon became hot NBA property. Barkley was one of just 11 players still registered that were selected by the NBA as one of the 50 all-time greats on the organisation's 50th birthday.

'Sir' Charles Barkley of the Houston Rockets.

LARRY BIRD

LARRY BIRD is one of the most famous names in basketball history. The Boston Celtic man joined the NBA in 1979–80 and in the 1980s picked up the MVP trophy three years running. Bird played in 10 All-Star games, picking up 79 rebounds and dishing out 41 assists. He was, in fact, an all-round player. For two seasons he led the NBA in three-point field goals and for four years he led the tables in free-throw shooting. Bird was part of a side that won the NBA Championships three times in the 1980s and in every one of those sides he was the leading scorer.

In NBA play-offs, he scored 1,458 goals, effected 296 steals (second only to 'Magic' Johnson) and delivered 1.062 assists (again only second to Johnson). He appeared in 164 play-off games. Bird's name became synonymous with basketball in the 1980s and he acted as a wonderful advertisement for the game throughout that period and beyond.

Larry Bird of the Celtics (right) during the 1990–91 season.

WILT 'THE STILT' CHAMBERLAIN

WILT 'THE STILT' Chamberlain was a member of the Harlem Globetrotters before joining the NBA with Philadelphia in 1959. At 2.2 m (7 ft 2 in) this giant was possibly the greatest basketball player ever. He is the only player to have scored over 100 points in a game. His scoring average is second only to Michael Jordan's, although Jordan's top score in a game is 69 and Chamberlain has topped that six times.

A five-times MVP, Chamberlain also holds records for the most field goals, most free throws and most rebounds in one game. For nine seasons he was the NBA's top scorer. Chamberlain played NBA basketball for 14 years, recording an average points tally of 30.1 per game. Like Jordan, Chamberlain was also a complete basketball player, leading the figures on a whole range of skills, including free throws and rebounds.

Wilt Chamberlain in 1976.

CHARLES 'TARZAN' COOPER

CHARLES 'TARZAN' COOPER was part of the all-conquering New York Renaissance side of the 1930s. Over a period of four years, the all-black Rens, which retained virtually the same line-up, won no less than 120 games per season while barnstorming. Cooper stood at 1.9 m (6 ft 5 in), one of only two six-footers on a team that relied on speed and teamwork to get results. The Rens were one of the biggest attractions in basketball in that era, and in 1939, with Cooper playing as a forward, they won the World Professional Basketball Tournament. After the break-up of the Rens, Cooper played guard for the Washington Bears and was part of their World Championship winning side in 1943. He was elected to the Hall of Fame in 1976.

BOB COUSEY

BOB COUSEY was part of the Boston Celtics side of the 1950s and 1960s. He was elected NBA MVP in 1956–57; that was in the middle of a run from 1952–60, during which he led the league in assists, a record eight seasons. Cousey's personal record was 28 assists in one game in 1959, and overall he dished out 6,955 assists. He was an All-Star player on 13 occasions. Cousey was another player who helped shape the game of basketball in the early years of the NBA. His contribution to the game was much greater than even his impressive statistics show and in 1970 he was elected to the Hall of Fame. He was a play-maker of the best quality and was one of the big attractions of the era.

The Boston Celtics, who have produced some of the finest players in the game over the years.

CLYDE 'THE GLIDE' DREXLER

CLYDE 'THE GLIDE' DREXLER was a supremely graceful basketball player who appeared to be able to steal the ball from an opponent at will. A long career would surely have produced better stats if he had played alongside the likes of Olajuwon. Playing for unfashionable Portland, Drexler made it to the All-Star games on eight occasions and in those games had a free-throw percentage bettered by

no one. In NBA finals he had a free-throw record of 78 from 93. In open play, Drexler's steal record put him amongst the top six all-time players and in January 1986 he effected 10 steals in one game. His elegance made him a popular player for neutrals to watch.

Drexler was never afraid to shoot from long-distance, making a creditable number of three-pointers. He also had an impressive assists record.

Clyde Drexler playing for the Houston Rockets in 1996.

BILL 'POP' GATES

BILL 'POP' GATES was another member of the barnstorming Renaissance side. He was one of the first black players to make it into pro-league basketball. While with the Rens, Gates would often play games twice a night. In 1946, Gates was one of two black players who broke into the National Basketball League (NBL), playing for Tri-Cities. By then he had already been part of World Championship sides with the Rens and the Washington Bears.

Gates became a legend in American basketball as a pioneer of the barnstorming days and for being a black player who broke into a white man's basketball league. He later went on to coach and was elected to the Hall of Fame in 1988 in recognition of his contribution to the development of the game.

The stadium at Washington, DC, home of Bill 'Pop' Gates's team, the Bears.

MARQUE HAYNES

BY THE TIME the Harlem Globetrotters played the World Champions, Minneapolis Lakers, in a two-game series in 1948, the side had already moved from straight basketball to exhibition play. Yet part of the prompting for such a venture was the fact that, for most of the time, the Globetrotters had no serious opposition. Marque Haynes was the greatest dribbler of that side. He would often sit down while still bouncing the ball and, when a steal was attempted, retain the ball before standing up to make a play. Haynes' ability was such that he could display such skills even when taking part in a prestigious 'serious' game against the World Champions. To be able to clown to the degree that Haynes did and still get results was the mark of a basketball genius. His fast and powerful dribbling technique was the inspiration for 'Magic' Johnson to take up basketball.

Today's Harlem Globetrotters, the team that made Haynes' name.

EARVIN 'MAGIC' JOHNSON

EARVIN 'MAGIC' JOHNSON was, like Michael Jordan, poetry in motion. His vision of a game was such that he really made things happen on a court. Johnson's speciality was the defence-splitting pass that would set up a team-mate for the score. A three-times MVP, Johnson is the only player to have registered over 1,000 assists in his career. His knack was not just to find the right player on the court with his pass, but to weight his pass to perfection, giving the receiver the best possible opportunity to use the ball. Johnson was not just an assist expert, however; in his first-ever NBA finals, he registered 42 points – a rookie record – when playing for Los Angeles in May 1980.

'Magic' Johnson playing for Los Angeles.

MICHAEL JORDAN

MICHAEL JORDAN burst on to the NBA basketball stage as Rookie of the Year in 1984–85 when he was Chicago's first draft pick. Since then he has become one of the most successful sportsmen the world has ever known.

He was a supreme athlete, whose skills on the court often led to him mesmerising his own team as well as the crowd and his opponents. A complete basketball player, he was the NBA's top points scorer from 1986–93 on a season-

Chicago Bulls' Michael Jordan.

by-season basis. He had scored more than 50 points in a game on no less than 26 occasions and had collected three MVPs before he announced his retirement in 1993 at the age of 30. He has picked up two more since coming out of retirement in 1995.

In a game dominated by statistics, however, they do not tell the full story of this amazing athlete. When Jordan came out of retirement, he re-joined the Chicago Bulls, where his on-field leadership took them straight to the NBA finals in his first full season back. Throughout his career, he has been an inspiration to a huge number of basketball players, young and old.

JOE LAPCHICK

HALL-OF-FAMER Joe Lapchick was a member of the 'Original Celtics', a barnstorming side from New York in the 1920s. Described at the time as 'elongated', Lapchick stood at 1.9 m (6 ft 5 in) tall at a time when basketball was not necessarily dominated by big men. A centre who was in great demand on the professional circuit, Lapchick formed part of the greatest side in the first half of the twentieth century. He was noted not only as a great all-round player with an exceptionally fine shot, but also as a team player who encouraged and got the best out of his team-mates. As a young man playing basketball at a time when earning a living at the game was hard, Lapchick would play owners off against each other for appearance money. His presence in a team would increase crowd attendances, making his fee worthwhile to owners.

MOSES MALONE

MOSES MALONE picked up three MVPs in the late 1970s, first with Houston, then with Philadelphia. A much-travelled player, he also wore the colours of Buffalo, Washington, Atlanta, Milwaukee and Boston. In 1983 he was the NBA finals MVP. He has played in 11 All-Star games and is an all-round player whose stats appear in the all-time top 10 for rebounds, free throws made and most games played. In fact, Malone's time at the top of the game compares with Kareem Abdul-Jabbar and Wilt Chamberlain's: only those two players have scored more points. Considered to be the most effective rebounder ever, Malone was the league's leading rebounder six times in the period 1978 to 1985. Malone was king of the boards at both ends of the court throughout his memorable career.

Moses Malone during the 1993–94 season.

HAKEEM OLAJUWON

POWER CENTRE Hakeem Olajuwon was a rookie in the same year as Michael Jordan, his early career being over-shadowed by the great guard. Nevertheless, Olajuwon has an impressive set of statistics. A regular All-Star player, he picked up his first MVP in 1993–94. That year he was also the finals MVP and picked up the Defensive Player of the Year award. A more rounded player than many think, Olajuwon can score and block with the best. His mere presence on court often causes a double-team that opens gaps for his team-mates. He was the main reason that the Houston Rockets won the NBA finals of 1994.

Nigerian-born Olajuwon is the complete defensive player, amongst the best at shot-blocking as well as rebounds. He also has an impressive record of steals in NBA finals.

Hakeem Olajuwon of the Houston Rockets.

SHAQUILLE O'NEAL

SHAQUILLE O'NEAL arrived in the NBA in the 1992–93 season, becoming Rookie of the Year with Orlando Magic. A 2.2 m (7 ft 2 in) colossus, he followed up the next year by being the NBA's top field-goal scorer, with an average of .599. O'Neal became famous for his 'Shaq Attack' slam dunk, leading some to believe that his only asset in basketball is his size and raw power. But O'Neal is a force to be reckoned with.

Shaquille O'Neal of the Lakers in 1997.

In his first year, his shot-blocking averaged 3.53 per game and he followed that up in 1993–94 with a year's stats that included 15 blocks in one game, 28 rebounds in another and 53 points in yet another.

O'Neal uses his size intelligently on court and is clearly more than just a big man.

SCOTTIE PIPPEN

SCOTTIE PIPPEN'S ability to read a game of basketball made him one of the most effective and most enjoyable players to watch. Pippen took over the mantle of leading the Chicago Bulls when Michael Jordan first retired. When he joined the Bulls in 1987, Pippen set straight to work learning his skills from Jordan. Pippen's basketballing brain ensured that he was able to pick up the lessons and become one of the best all-round basketball players ever. When Jordan retired in 1993, Pippen led the Bulls in scoring, assists and steals, effecting nine steals in one game that season.

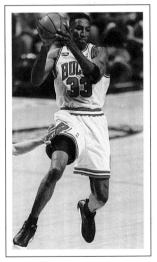

Once Jordan returned to Chicago the two matched up and, joined by Rodman, became the most compelling force in modern basketball history.

Scottie Pippen, Michael Jordan's Chicago team-mate.

OSCAR 'BIG O' ROBERTSON

OSCAR 'BIG O' ROBERTSON'S record of assists is bettered only by 'Magic' Johnson. He was the NBA Rookie of the Year in 1960, collecting the MVP in the 1963–64 season. Playing for Cincinnati for 10 years before switching to Milwaukee, he was a 12-times NBA All-Stars player, holding a 20.5 scoring record in All-Star games. Over his career, Robertson averaged 9.5 assists per game.

Robertson's other speciality was the free throw. He led the league free-throw stats in four seasons. In December 1964, he hit 22 from 26 for Cincinnati against Baltimore and 22 from 23 against Los Angeles. In 1963 he also hit 21 from 22 in a play-off game for Cincinnati against Boston in the Eastern Division final.

DENNIS 'BAD BOY' RODMAN

DENNIS 'BAD BOY' RODMAN is the greatest self-publicist in modern sport. Yet behind this image is a truly great basketball player. Chicago coach Phil Jackson gambled on taking an unreliable and possibly over-aged Rodman into his side in 1995 to team him up with Michael Jordan and co. By that time Rodman had already hit the record books with the most rebounds in one game (32). He had been the NBA's top rebounder four years running from 1990–94, a record beaten only by Moses Malone.

Moving to Chicago to play with Pippen and Jordan, Rodman became an even better player, picking up the winners' medals to prove it. Rodman the individualist had found a team that he could fit into, harnessing his huge potential to the delight of basketball fans everywhere.

Dennis Rodman, known as 'Bad Boy'.

Star of the 1950s and '60s Bill Russell.

BILL RUSSELL

AT THE DAWN of professional basketball, Bill Russell of the Boston Celtics was the man who changed the entire method of defence. His block was considered by contemporaries to be possibly the best, but in statistical terms it was his rebounding that goes down in history.

Russell, as a five times MVP, was part of the Boston set-up that dominated basketball throughout the 1950s and early 1960s. His rebounding stats are second only to Chamberlain's, and it can be argued that he was the most influential player in basketball at the time. Even in the NBA play-offs, against top opposition, Russell's rebounding stats include 40 in one game twice – first in 1958 then again in 1960. In total Russell picked off 21,620 rebounds in a career that included 12 appearances in All-Star teams.

JERRY WEST

HALL-OF-FAMER Jerry West had a career that spanned 14 years in the NBA. His defensive skills were so admired that for three consecutive seasons he was elected by coaches to the All-Defensive team. He was also MVP for the NBA finals of 1969; yet West made his mark in more than just his defensive role. He scored a total of 9,016 field goals at a time when basketball was not considered to be a sport just for big men. In fact, West was the man who perfected the jump shot, which became a regular part of the basketball-players' armoury.

Playing in the same side as Wilt Chamberlain, West was also responsible for a large number of assists, his work often benefiting Chamberlain.

Top 10 Players in the Rest of the World

(NATIONALITY GIVEN IN BRACKETS)

ALTON BYRD (USA)

ALTON BYRD came to Britain in 1979, with two MVPs already under his belt – a feat that he repeated in his first two years in British basketball with Crystal Palace. Byrd, a 1.7 m (5 ft 8 in) guard, has since won every honour there is in British basketball. He led Crystal Palace to a unique triple success in his first year and was clearly better than any other British-based player. He was capped 18 times for England.

Living proof that skill and agility are as important as size in basketball, Byrd was an ambassador for the game, and over the years, first as a player then as a coach, he was been the most significant player in the country. His career stats include 1,778 assists in the British game. Despite his size, Byrd could drive to the basket with the best.

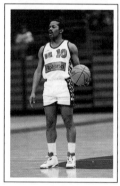

Britain's Alton Byrd.

PREDRAG DANILOVIC (YUGOSLAVIA)

PREDRAG DANILOVIC has played in the NBA with Dallas and that experience has given his defensive game a much harder edge. On top of this, he is without question one of the best offensive players in Europe and can always be relied upon to make a crucial shot count. The Yugoslav international displays genuine all-round talents during a game and, apart from being a superb shooter, can drive and dump brilliantly. He is a coach's dream performer on the court – a player with outstanding individual skills, who is also always an excellent team player. The 2.03 m (6 ft 8 in) forward was unlucky enough to miss out on his country's 1998 World Basketball Championship success because of an injury. He currently plays for Kinder Virtus Bologna in the Italian A-1 League.

Yugoslavia's Predrag Danilovic.

SASHA DANILOVIC
(YUGOSLAVIA)

NICKNAMED 'THE TERMINATOR', Sasha Danilovic is an all-round basketball player who will play both offence and defence. He was elected Europe's top defensive player, but is also happy driving to the basket, drawing fouls. He has won Olympic, World, European and national medals and has won the Euroleague with two different sides: Partizan and Kinder Bologna. He has also held the European MVP.

At 2.03 m (6 ft 8 in) Danilovic is a forward who wins games. His decision-making is second to none and there can be little doubt that he is good enough to play NBA basketball.

His stats for 1997–98 give him a points tally of 21.8, and beyond that his Offensive Efficiency Rating was an impressive 1.10 – in other words, when Danilovic got the ball his side nearly always scored.

Yugoslavia's Sasha Danilovic.

ALEKSANDAR 'SALE' DJORDJEVIC (YUGOSLAVIA)

CURRENTLY PLAYING FOR Barcelona, Aleksandar 'Sale' Djordjevic was reportedly the highest-paid player in Spain's Liga ACB during the 1997–98 season. He never quite made it when he tried his luck in the NBA, but on the European scene he is certainly one of the stars.

The 1.87 m (6 ft 2 in) guard helped Yugoslavia win the gold medal at the 1998 World Basketball Championships and had an excellent game in the final, when his country beat Russia 64-62.

Djordjevic shows great vision on the court and is a great driver, especially on the left. He is a brilliant three-point shooter. Djordjevic, who won the Euroleague with Partizan in 1992, has a lot of experience and uses it well.

Aleksandar Djordjevic of Yugoslavia.

Toni Kukoc of Croatia.

TONI KUKOC (CROATIA)

TONI KUKOC joined the NBA with the Chicago Bulls in 1993, but was a highly successful international player before then. In fact, the Bulls selected forward Kukoc as their second pick in 1990, but he decided to stay in Europe for a further two years with Benetton Treviso of Italy.

Prior to his stint in Italy, Kukoc had already won three consecutive European Cup Winners' medals with Yugoplastika Split. The 2.1 m (6 ft 11 in) powerhouse is a determined and awkward player, who has at times been underestimated; yet his longevity with the most successful Bulls side ever is a statement in itself. Kukoc will be playing in the NBA until 2000, but as a European it is possible that he could return to Europe to finish his career.

MARCELO NICOLA (SPAIN–ARGENTINA)

MARCELO NICOLA is said to be on a lucrative four-year contract with his club Barcelona, which is worth $2.6 million. However, the 1997–98 season proved unsuccessful for the Spanish Liga ACB side and, indeed, their star player Marcelo Nicola.

The Spanish-Argentinian has been accused of lacking concentration and intensity on the court, but the 2.08 m (6 ft 10 in) forward clearly has the skills, athleticism and strength to be rated one of the best players in the world not playing in the NBA. He is a good three-point shooter, draws plenty of fouls and uses his body and height well. The enigmatic forward still has it in him to silence the critics if only he can regain the consistency required and prove his worth to the country.

DINO RADJA (CROATIA)

DINO RADJA was a key player for his club Panathinaikos (Athens) when they won the 1997–98 Greek A-1 League Championship title. For his endeavours, the Croat centre was named runner-up in the League's MVP nominations.

He has been courted by NBA clubs on several occasions and spent some time with Boston. However, he remains in Europe, and deservedly retains his status as one of the most gifted performers not playing in the United States.

Radja has first-class skills, movement and vision on court. He has worked hard on his low game in recent seasons and is unstoppable one-on-one. Radja, who stands 2.1 m (6 ft 11 in) tall, is also a brilliant jumper facing the basket.

Croatian Dino Radja.

ZELIKO REBRACA (YUGOSLAVIA)

ZELIKO REBRACA spear-headed Yugoslavia's charge to the 1998 World Basketball Championship title. He had 16 points and 11 rebounds in his country's 64-62 victory over Russia in the final. He is a very athletic player with a full range of natural basketball skills and is especially dangerous near the opposition's basket. Rebraca has always been a great attacking talent and now that he is showing increased toughness in defence, he is without doubt one of the best players in Europe – and there is still some time for further improvement. The centre plays for Benetton Treviso in the highly competitive Italian A-1 League and will want to keep his form and fitness together for the 2000 Olympic Games in Sydney.

Zeliko Rebraca, now playing in Italy.

ZORAN SAVIC (YUGOSLAVIA)

ZORAN SAVIC is one of basketball's toughest competitors and as a result has won more honours in the European game than most other players. He has been known to play on after being injured and still totally dominate a game. Savic's defensive skills may not be the best in the land but his attacking play can be devastating. His assets are his brain and

heart. The Yugoslav may not be the most athletic or the fastest player on the court, but his know-how and will to win make him a true champion.

The 2.08 m (6 ft 10 in) centre plays for Kinder Virtus Bologna in the Italian A-1 League, which itself is rated one of the toughest leagues outside the United States.

Zoran Savic of Yugoslavia.

DOMINIQUE WILKINS
(USA)

DOMINIQUE WILKINS was born in the United States and was a prolific points scorer in the NBA during the early part of his basketball career in his native country. The 2.03 m (6 ft 8 in) forward has a reputation for being unpredictable on the court, but when he is on song he is spectacular. He currently plays for Teamsystem Fortitudo Bologna in the Italian A-1 League, where he is said to be on a two-year, $4-million contract.

Now very much in the veteran class, Wilkins remains one of the best players in one of the strongest leagues outside the NBA. Success in Europe has seen him win the Euroleague with Panathinaikos (Athens) and the Italy Cup with Teamsystem Fortitudo Bologna in 1998.

American-born Dominique Wilkins.

Players to Watch in the Future

KOBE BRYANT (USA)

KOBE BRYANT is already being labelled as the new Michael Jordan; the truth is he is a phenomenally good player in his own right. Bryant is the son of top-quality NBA player and coach Joe Bryant, and is already a complete player at the age of 21. He is the youngest All-Star player in the history of the game and set a record for being the youngest NBA player, after turning professional at the age of 17. At high schools, Bryant was simply unstoppable as a play-maker and point-scorer, giving the appearance of a pro amongst amateurs. Since joining the NBA, Bryant has earned the praise of Michael Jordan, who recognises something of himself in the young man. Bryant has established himself as a quality player in the strongest basketball league in the world. His dedication to the sport guarantees that he will get even better – an awesome prospect for opponents.

Michael Jordan, who has recognised some of his own talent in the young Kobe Bryant.

YORICK WILLIAMS (GREAT BRITAIN)

YORICK WILLIAMS is a 1.93 m (6 ft 4 in) Mancunian who signed for his local side, Manchester Giants, making his debut in 1994. In 1995 he won the Slam Dunk Championship before going to America to develop his game in 1996. Returning to play for Derby Storm, Williams is a stylish guard who has clearly benefited from being in the United States. His ability and confidence when driving to the basket make him a delight to watch, even when playing in a league dominated by Americans. Williams is also a confident free-throw shooter, whose early stats showed a great promise. He is a clear thinker who remains calm under pressure, and on his return to England he immediately became top scorer and top three-point shooter with Derby, as well as leading the team's three-throw percentage table. With little doubt, Yorick Williams is an All-Star of the future in the making.

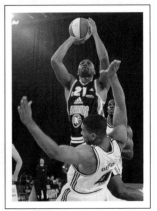

Yorick Williams' original team the Manchester Giants, playing London Towers.

BECOMING A PLAYER

How and Where to Start

In the United States everybody loves and plays basketball. You can see baskets everywhere: in the garden, on the garage wall, in fact anywhere there is space to run and jump at the ring. It is seen as a natural process for any small child, having learnt to walk, to want to learn how to pass, dribble, drive and shoot the ball at the basket.

YOUNGSTERS IN THE United States are actively encouraged to take up the sport. There will be basketball facilities at every high school and college, plus local leagues in most American cities and towns. If you are born in the home of the NBA, you are thought to be quite unusual if you don't like or want to play basketball at some level.

The pick-up game – spontaneous matches usually played outside in public areas – is a phenomenon in

Youth basketball.

the United States and has attracted its own set of rules, language and fashion. In short, if you are an American, you don't have to ask the question how and where can you take up basketball – you just start playing.

The popularity of basketball has spread rapidly around the world, especially after the appearance of the American Dream Team at the 1992 Barcelona Olympics – a side that included such great and inspirational players as Michael Jordan, 'Magic' Johnson and Larry Bird.

Developments in satellite and cable television services have seen NBA games frequently broadcast throughout the world, and this helps keep alive the enthusiasm for the sport.

With the advent of digital broadcasting just around the corner, planet Earth can look forward to yet more televised coverage of the fastest-growing sport in the world.

Larry Bird playing for the Boston Celtics.

Playing Facilities

Basketball is no longer a minority sport in many countries and as a result, playing and coaching facilities are becoming more readily available. In Britain, most sports centres and gyms would have at least one court – many would have indoor and outdoor playing areas. It is almost standard practice nowadays for schools and colleges to have some sort of basketball playing facility.

THE PICK-UP game in some of the inner-urban areas of Britain's big cities has started to take off, but it certainly is not as astonishingly popular in Britain as it is in the United States.

Basketball still draws larger crowds in the US than it does in Britain.

However, because basketball is such a simple sport and requires just a ball and a basket to play the game, it is easy to practice on your own or with a few friends. This is how many young players get a feel for the game, and if they enjoy it they can join a properly constituted basketball club – one that has organised matches and experienced coaches.

The big increase in demand for the provision of basketball courts in Britain, caused by the game's rapid development, has seen many more playing areas provided. The sports clothing and equipment manufacturer, adidas, have recently agreed with a number of local councils to provide open-air hoops in parks and public open spaces. Britain is certainly not as basketball crazy as the United States, but any young Briton wishing to take up the sport does not have to search high and low for a chance as they might have done 20 years ago.

Basketball can be played anywhere, with just a hoop and ball.

Kit Requirements

The individual's kit for basketball is quite simply a vest, shorts, socks and footwear.

VEST

IN ORGANISED MATCHES all players on the same team should wear the same colour outfit and be clearly distinguishable from the opposition. The club will usually provide the clothing for these matches. The rules state that each player must have a number clearly marked on their vest, and that no two in a team should display the same number.

The number on the front of the vest should be 10 cm (4 in) high and the one on the back

All players on the same team should wear the same colour vest.

20 cm (8 in) high. FIBA shirts are numbered 4–15 while the NBA allows other combinations. In addition, numbers 20–25, 30–35, 40–45, and 50–55 are sometimes used in local leagues. Some players prefer to wear a T-shirt under their vest for added comfort and this should be the same colour as the vest.

SHORTS

SHORTS SHOULD BE loose-fitting for comfort and mobility and the same colour as the vest. Players who wear long undershorts are also required by some leagues to match the colour of the undershorts to their shorts. As with other well-marketed and televised sports such as soccer, fashions come and go in basketball. In recent years shorts have become longer and baggier: a trend started by the great player, Michael Jordan.

There are strict rules about the size of numbers on vests.

FOOTWEAR

FOOTWEAR IS PROBABLY the most important part of a
player's equipment because of the pounding the feet take
during the course of a match. Basketball shoes can be either
high or low cut, depending on the player's personal choice. The
shoes should be rubber-soled with protected ankle supports,

Footwear is the most important part of a player's kit.

and players in the same team are usually required by leagues to wear the same basic colour shoes – very often black or white.

They should be comfortable to wear and have a sole thick enough to cushion the strain of jumping and landing on the feet. It is often advisable to wear towelling socks to reduce the risk of getting blisters. Some players prefer to buy shoes that would normally be a little too big for them so they can wear two pairs of socks. One tip is to buy your shoes late in the day when your feet may have swollen slightly. They are likely to swell as a result of the rigours of a basketball match, so don't try on new shoes in the morning. Another tip is to lace your shoes up tightly as if you were about to start a match and jog around the store. Make certain that both feet feel comfortable.

Boots should have thick rubber soles and ankle supports.

PROTECTIVE KIT

VIRTUALLY ALL PLAYERS wear mouthguards for protection during games – one of the most notable players being the NBA's Charles Barkley. These protect a player's mouth from flying elbows and are particularly useful if a player is constantly crashing into the boards for rebounds. Goggles can also be worn to prevent eye injuries.

Watches and jewellery can cause injuries, and most leagues have rules banning players from wearing them during matches. If you are playing in a casual game of basketball try not to wear shirts with buttons – these can get caught on other players and cause injury.

Players often wear protective goggles or mouthguards.

STREET FASHION

AS WITH THE baseball cap, items of basketball clothing have become fashion items, with shoes and socks leading the way. Basketball shoes are worn by millions as normal casual footwear, while socks have given rise to a number of fads. Ankle socks similar to those worn by tennis players are *de rigueur* in the sport nowadays.

Michael Jordan started yet another trend a few years ago when he began wearing black socks. Almost immediately black socks were being worn not just by Jordan's fellow NBA professionals, but also players of every standard throughout the United States.

Scottie Pippen sporting the new trend for black socks.

Equipment

BALL

THE BALL SHOULD be spherical, of an approved orange colour, have an outer surface of leather, rubber or synthetic material, and have seams which do not exceed 6.35 mm (0.25 in). Its circumference must measure between 74.9 and 78 cm (11.5 and 12 in) and it should weigh between 567 and 650 g (20 and 22 oz). Its air pressure should ensure that, when dropped from 1.80 m (5.4 ft) on to the playing surface, it will rebound to a height between 1.20 and 1.40 m (3.5 and 4 ft). The home team should provide at least two balls which conform to the above specifications. The referee will be the sole judge of a ball's legality.

Circumference between 74.9 and 78 cm (11.5 and 12 in)

BACKBOARDS

BACKBOARDS ARE generally made of hardwood, although pro-ball uses glass backboards. They should each be 3 cm (1.1 in) thick, 1.80 m (5.4 ft) across and 1.05 m (3.1 ft) high, with the lower edge 2.90 m (8.8 ft) above the floor. The front surface should be flat and all lines should be white if the backboard is transparent, and black otherwise. The backboards, which should be brightly coloured in contrast with their background so that they are clearly visible to the players, are mounted at right angles to the floor and parallel to the endlines. The bottom and sides of the backboard, and the backboard supports, must all be padded with a minimum thickness of 5 cm (2 in).

BASKETS

BASKETS COMPRISE rings and nets. The rings, painted orange and made of solid iron, have a diameter of 45 cm (17 in). They are attached horizontally to the backboards 3.05 m (10 ft) above the floor and the inside point of the ring should be no nearer to the face of the backboard than 15 cm (6 in). The nets, between 40 and 45 cm (15 and 17 in) long, are made of white cord suspended from the rings.

Official baskets are made to specific measurements.

TECHNICAL EQUIPMENT

THE HOME SIDE must also provide officials with game clocks and scoreboards, which should be visible to everyone involved with the game, and a stopwatch for timing time-outs. A 30-second device is needed to count down the seconds digitally when the 30-second rule is in operation.

At least two separate pieces of signalling equipment are required so that the end of a period, half and game can be sounded, so that officials can be alerted to time-out requests during a dead-ball period, and that the end of a 30-second period can be signalled. An official FIBA-approved scoresheet is filled in by the scorer, who also looks after the player foul markers, which are white and rectangular, and team foul markers, which are red and usually triangular.

The final piece of required equipment is a team fouls indicator, which keeps count of the fouls committed by the teams and indicates when they have reached penalty status.

Scoreboards, clocks etc., should be visible to everyone involved in the game.

Fitness Tips

The most important thing to remember when training and practising for basketball is to use the ball as much as possible. This will help develop your handling skills with the ball.

S KILL AND PHYSICAL fitness are the two key ingredients that make up a successful and, crucially, sustainable basketball career. However, it is no good being able to do all kinds of magic tricks with the ball if your body is unable to cope with the physical demands made on it by the game.

Basketball is a team game, but individuals can practise on their own, so long as they have a ball, basket and a wall to

Always be guided by the coach's advice and help.

bounce the ball off. An individual can also keep fit with a personal fitness programme.

If you are a serious team player, you should try to train with your club as often as possible, not only to take advantage of the club facilities, but also to take part in organised training sessions. This will help all aspects of your team play and also help test your level of fitness against other players of your own age or ability.

Take note of every word of advice by the club coaching staff – you are never too old to learn. The club coach will be responsible for organising training sessions. Different coaches have differing views on training of course, but most sessions will involve exercises (or drills) which are designed to improve a specific individual skill. These sessions will involve repeated practice of a certain skill which players can practise on their own away from the club.

Above: keeping fit is crucial to success as a player.

Where to Train

Every member of a basketball team has to shoot. It is essential that all players – especially those new to the game – should practise shooting as much as possible. If you have a back garden, it would be useful if you could instal a basket to assist your practising. Don't always shoot from the same spot, and vary the style of shot you make.

A T EVERY OPPORTUNITY, practise all the skills required in basketball – at your club, back garden or the local sports centre or gymnasium. The sports centre or gymnasium will be a great place to train. It will no doubt have a basketball court marked out and baskets to attack and defend. Go with friends and enjoy the more relaxed atmosphere of training on court rather than at your club. However, even in these more casual sessions always practise your skills seriously.

Take even the most casual sessions seriously, always warming up properly.

The sports centre or gymnasium will also have the facilities to help improve your physical fitness. A trainer may be able to draw up a personal fitness programme for you, which involves using some of the gym's equipment.

Wherever you train for basketball, try to enjoy the sessions – hard work in the gym will dovetail nicely with the individual skill drills to make you a better all-round player.

Get into practice at your local sports centre or gym.

TRAINING FOR JUNIOR PLAYERS

DURING THE LAST 20 years, toy manufacturers have been selling baskets and basketballs suitable for use by extremely young children. The baskets are set much lower to the ground and the balls have been made of soft materials such as sponge, so that they can be played within the home without causing damage. As a consequence, a large number of children who are keen to start playing organised basketball at the age of 11 have a basic feel for the game already and know all the skills required to be a good player, without having honed them on a full-size court.

Children at that age are, of course, still growing, and it may be difficult to assess which players have it in them to develop into good all-round players. Some children may be big for their age and take advantage of their height, weight and strength. Therefore, training for players of this age should be all about developing skills – again that means practise, practise and more practise. However, it has to be made enjoyable for the young player.

For the under-14s it is vital that winning matches is not the main

Find a local club for under-14s to start practising.

purpose of being on a basketball court. It has to be fun and they should be encouraged to continue to develop their love of the game until the more serious training starts at 14-plus.

Players may still be developing physically up to the age of 18 or 19, and basketball training for teenagers should see them start to play serious league and cup matches where victory is important. As ever, they should be encouraged to improve their skills and fitness, but it is at this age that tactics should start to be taught.

The maxim of many coaches of younger players is: keep it simple, make it fun.

It is essential to keep youth basketball fun.

Weight Training and Diet

Physical fitness is vital if you want to be a successful player, as basketball demands a lot of a player's body. Strength, speed and agility are essential requirements.

A GOOD WAY OF building up your strength and muscle power is to set up your own fitness programme and ensure it includes allocated time for specialised weight training. Full fitness not only helps make you a better player, it also reduces the risk of injury.

There has been something of a revolution recently in the thinking on sport and diet. Fatty foods such as red meat are out and low-fat foods are in. A balanced diet should include lots of

Michael Olowokandi keeping fit.

fruits, vegetables and whole grains; a meal before a match should be eaten three to four hours before it starts. A good pre-game meal should contain foods that have high-carbohydrate sources such as pasta and cereals. The body can convert the calories into energy in time for the start of the match. Fatty foods remain in the digestive tract for much longer and will make you feel sluggish.

AVOIDING AND TREATING INJURIES

ALTHOUGH BASKETBALL IS supposed to be a non-contact sport, injuries do occur. Kit, such as goggles and mouthguards can help prevent knocks. Blisters are a common problem and good socks and shoes can assist in keeping them at bay. A sprained ankle is the most common form of injury in basketball and many top players tape their ankles before every match to help keep them stable. If you are injured during a match, get someone to assess the severity of it immediately. Don't play on with a bad injury: a torn muscle can keep you out of the game for a long time, especially if you have damaged it further by spending another few minutes on the court.

Good shoes and socks can prevent a number of serious injuries.

Where to Find Clubs

With the popularity of basketball growing every year, more and more basketball clubs are being formed. The number of league competitions has increased considerably in the last five years and as a result, more and more young people are taking up basketball than ever before.

BASKETBALL MAY BE on your school or college sports programme and you are participating in matches already. The matches may be organised on a friendly basis or played as part of a league structure. A local amateur club, or indeed one of the professional clubs, may have an association with your school or college and it should be easy for you find out more about becoming a member.

Many schools and colleges have basketball programmes.

If you are starting from scratch, the local public library will have a list of all the basketball clubs in your area – or may even have an advertisement on their noticeboard by a basketball club encouraging new members to join.

Your local sports centre may have one or two clubs regularly playing on their courts. Enquire at the desk to see if a name and number can be obtained. Contact the local office of the Sports Council, who will provide details of clubs and facilities in your area.

You can also contact the English Basketball Association (EBBA), who will provide a list of clubs affiliated to their organisation.

Local college basketball.

Becoming a Referee

> The referee is the most senior match official in
> basketball. He will be assisted by an umpire, a
> scorer, a timekeeper and, in top-class games, a
> 30-second operator.

T HE REFEREE AND UMPIRE jointly control the game
and take up positions on opposite sides of the courts, in
order to see all the action. They swap sides before each jump-
ball and after each foul. The referee and umpire must wear long
dark trousers, a grey or black and white shirt and black
basketball shoes. This ensures that they are easily distinguishable from the players.

The referee's word is the law during a game.

The duties of a referee include: putting the ball into play; ordering time-outs; giving the ball to a player for a specified throw and confirming the position of the throw. He will also stop play when the ball is 'dead'. The referee has ultimate control and his word is final. Crucially, the referee is responsible for imposing penalties when the rules are breached and for unsportsmanlike behaviour. As the senior official, the referee is also responsible for the inspection and approval of all equipment.

Both the referee and umpire use a series of hand signals to indicate their decisions to the players, the off-court officials and spectators. A good referee must know the rules of the game thoroughly and always be in the right position at the right time to see the play.

A young person wishing to become a basketball referee should study the movements and signals of the officials at matches. Put yourself in their place and see if you come to the same decisions.

The EBBA runs various courses for match officials and it is through the governing body that you will eventually earn your referee's badge.

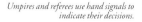

Umpires and referees use hand signals to indicate their decisions.

Becoming a Coach

All good basketball coaches are keen students of the game and never stop trying to gain more knowledge about the sport. If you want to become a coach and have not played much competitive basketball yourself, learn the basics of the game by watching as many live matches as possible. Study video recordings of games and talk to as many people with experience as possible. Join a local club and get involved in as many activities as you can.

I F YOU ARE ALREADY a player and are thinking of becoming a coach, ask to help out with your team's training sessions. You may be required to help out with the younger players, who are learning the basic skills of the sport.

The EBBA publish a number of coaching manuals and videos. They also organise courses for

Larry Bird in his role as Pacer's coach.

coaches and award official coaching certificates to successful participants. Contact them and see if there is a course available to meet your requirements.

Although basketball is basically a simple game, many different elements can decide the outcome of a game and the coach must therefore be ready to switch tactics, make substitutions and cajole his players during the hectic periods of play. Be prepared to have to think quickly on your feet. The pressure may be intense, but the pleasures of coaching, not just successful teams, but developing the skills of young players, can be immense.

A good coach must encourage and cajole his team during a match.

RULES OF THE GAME

Rules – A Beginner's Guide

THE TEAM

BASKETBALL IS played between two sides. Each team can
consist of up to 10 players, but only five players from each side
are allowed to play at any given moment.

THE COURT

THE GAME IS played on a court marked on a flat surface –
grass courts are not used for organised matches.

A team can have up to 10 members, although only five can play at one time.

THE GOAL

THE AIM OF both sides is to score more goals than the opposition. A goal (or basket) is scored when the ball enters the basket from above. The basket is fixed 3.05 m (10 ft) above the floor. Goals can be worth one, two or three points depending on the circumstances. A goal from a free-throw (given when a player is fouled) is worth one point. Goals scored in open play from outside a semi-circle marked from the basket are worth three points. Goals scored from within the semi-circle are worth two points.

LENGTH OF THE GAME

THE GAME IS divided into two halves of 20 minutes each. If the scores are level at the end of normal time, an extra period of five minutes is played. If the scores remain the same, further periods are played until a winning team emerges.

Games are controlled by a referee and an umpire, who are assisted by a scorer and a timekeeper.

A goal is scored when the ball enters the basket from above.

MOVEMENT OF THE BALL

TO ADVANCE UP the court a player may dribble the ball by bouncing it to the ground with one hand. When a player ends a dribble, he must do it within the limits of two steps. A player can not run with the ball in his hands. The other options available to move the ball are to pass it to a team-mate or shoot for the basket.

FOULS

BASKETBALL IS supposed to be a non-contact sport and fouls are awarded if a player impedes another. This violation is known as a personal foul. Technical fouls are given for an infringement against the spirit of the rules or the use of un-sportsmanlike tactics.

Dribbling the ball is the most popular way of advancing up the court.

POSITIONS

THERE ARE NO restrictions on where a player can position themselves on court. All five players are expected to attack and defend as required.

POSSESSION OF THE BALL

THERE ARE A NUMBER of time rules in basketball which were introduced to stop negative play. A team in possession of the ball must try for a basket within 30 seconds of getting it. When a team takes control of the ball in their own half of the court, they must move it into their opponent's half within 10 seconds. If the ball goes out of play and a side is awarded a throw-in, the ball must be put back into play within five seconds.

To summarise, basketball is a simple game and no physical contact is allowed. There are restrictions on how you can move the ball around the court and there are time rules to obey. You score points by dropping the ball into the opposition's basket. You win the match if you score more points than the other team.

All players are both attackers and defenders.

Rules – Further Details

COURT DIMENSIONS

FOR COMPETITIONS under the jurisdiction of the sport's governing body FIBA (*Federation Internationale de Basketball*), a court should be 28 m (85 ft) long and 15 m (49 ft) wide measured from the inside edge of the boundary line. Smaller courts can be used for other matches, provided they are no less than 24 m (72 ft) long and 13 m (39 ft) wide. Any reduction in size must be in proportion. The height of the ceiling or lowest overhead obstruction must be at least 7 m (21 ft) and the court should be uniformly lighted. The court's lines should all be 5 cm (2 in) wide, the same colour and completely visible. The lines along the sides of the court are called sidelines and the lines defining each end are called endlines.

A centre line parallel to the endlines bisects the court and extends 15 cm (6 in) beyond each sideline. The free throw lines are 3.6 m (11 ft) long and 5.8 m (17 ft) in court from the endlines. Their central points lie on an imaginary line joining the central points of the two endlines. The restricted areas are defined by free-throw lanes drawn from the ends of the free-throw lines to 3 m (9 ft), either side of the central point of the endlines.

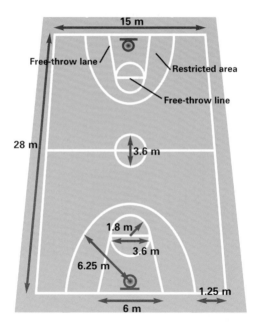

Free-throw lane

Restricted area

Free-throw line

15 m

28 m

3.6 m

1.8 m

3.6 m

6.25 m

6 m

1.25 m

The official court at the Barcelona Olympics in 1992.

The free-throw lanes are extended into the playing court by a semi-circle with a radius of 1.8 m (5.4 ft) and a similar semi-circle is marked by a broken line within each restricted area. The restricted areas are enclosed in another area, which starts within 1.25 m (3.8 ft) of each end of the endlines,

extends out with lines parallel to the sidelines before forming another semi-circle with a radius of 6.25 m (19 ft) from the centre of the basket.

The centre circle, bisected by the centre line, has a diameter of 3.6 m (5.4 ft) measured to the outer edge of its circumference. Team bench areas are marked out, 9 m (27 ft) long and 2 m (6 ft) wide, on separate sides of the scorer's table.

Match Officials and Team Personnel

The referee and umpire, assisted by a timekeeper, scorer, assistant scorer and 30-second operator, will ensure the game is played according to FIBA rules. Sometimes a technical commissioner will supervise the table officials (timekeepers and scorers).

REFEREE AND UMPIRE

THE REFEREE AND umpire must wear a grey or black and white shirt and black trousers, shoes and socks. The referee must approve all equipment to be used during a game and should not allow players to wear dangerous objects.

He starts the game with a jump ball, has the power to stop play and has the final decision on all matters.

The referee must wear grey, black and white to distinguish himself from the players.

The officials' powers start 20 minutes before a game and terminate when the referee signs the scoresheet at the end. It is also the referee's responsibility to report any protests by either side to the appropriate authority.

When a violation is committed, the referee or umpire blows a whistle and signals for the clock to be stopped and then awards a throw-in. When a personal foul occurs, the referee or umpire indicates to the offender that a foul has been committed and reports it to the scorer's table. After each foul or decision which results in a jump-ball restart, the officials should exchange their positions on court.

The referee indicates when a foul has been committed.

When a player commits a foul, the scorer indicates with a marker the number of fouls committed by that player.

SCORER

THE SCORER KEEPS a record of the players who start the game, monitors all the substitutions and maintains a chronological summary of points scored, field goals and free throws. He or she keeps a note of the personal and technical fouls called on each player and should notify the referee immediately after the fifth foul in games of two 20-minute periods or the sixth foul in games of four 12-minute periods. Also, the scorer logs the technical fouls called on each coach and notifies the referee as soon as a coach must leave the game; records the time-outs taken by each team and notifies the coach through an official when he has taken a second time-out in 2 x 20-minute games or third time-out in 4 x 12-minute games. He or she signals to the officials when the timekeeper indicates that a time-out has lasted 50 seconds.

Every time a player commits a foul, the scorer raises a marker showing the number of that player's fouls. In 2 x 20-minute games, a red marker should be placed on the scorer's table once a team has committed its seventh foul in one period, or its fourth foul in one period in 4 x 12-minute games. The assistant scorer's main task is to operate the scoreboard.

TIMEKEEPER

THE TIMEKEEPER keeps a record of playing time and stoppages, and should notify the referee more than three minutes before the end of a period so he can notify the teams. At time-outs, the timekeeper stops the watch and directs the scorer to signal when 50 seconds have elapsed. At the end of each period, the timekeeper must stop the clock and sound a loud signal. The 30-second operator's duty is to operate the 30-second device.

PLAYERS, SUBSTITUTES AND COACHES

EACH TEAM consists of not more than 10 players for 2 x 20-minute games or 12 for 4 x 12-minute games or tournaments involving more than three games, plus a coach and, perhaps, an assistant coach. Only five players from each team can be on court at one time and all players must wear a number on their shirts.

Captains are allowed to address an official on court to obtain essential information when the ball is dead. If the captain leaves the court, he must inform the referee which player is replacing him as captain. At least 20 minutes before the game, the coach must hand the scorer a team list which gives the players' names and numbers, and identifies the captain, coach and assistant coach.

Extra players in the team awaiting their turn on court.

The five players to start the game should be confirmed at least 10 minutes beforehand, and when a substitution is made the player coming on must report to the scorer first. Only the coach is allowed to stand during the game or communicate with the table officials when the ball is dead.

Head coach for the Indiana Pacers, Larry Bird, at the 1998 NBA play-offs.

Timing Regulations

LENGTH OF EACH GAME

EACH GAME CONSISTS OF two 20-minute halves or four 12-minute quarters with two minute intervals between the first and second, and the third and fourth periods. The half-time break should last either 10 or 15 minutes.

The game clock starts when the jump ball is tapped by a player after reaching its highest point on the toss, when the ball

The scoreboard at St Petersburg in Florida.

stays in play after an unsuccessful free throw, and when the ball touches a player following a throw-in. The clock should stop at the end of a half or period and when the whistle is blown or the 30-second signal is sounded.

THE 30-SECOND RULE

UNDER THE 30-second rule, when a player gains control of the ball, his team must attempt a shot within 30 seconds unless they lose possession. Failure to do this will result in the sounding of the 30-second signal. The 30-second device will be stopped, but not reset, if an injured player needs treatment or the ball has gone out of bounds and the side in possession has a throw-in.

A team must attempt a shot at goal within 30 seconds of gaining possession of the ball.

THE TIME-OUT

TIME-OUTS CAN LAST a maximum of one minute, with two per half allowed in 2 x 20-minute games and three per half allowed in 4 x 12-minute games. Only one time-out is allowed in each period of extra-time, and unused time-outs cannot be carried over to the next half or extra-time. If the team responsible for the time-out is ready to play before a minute is up, the referee should restart the game as soon as possible. During a time-out, players are allowed to leave the court and sit on their team bench. Time-out requests are made in person to the scorer by either the coach or his assistant. The scorer sounds the signal and the timekeeper stops the clock as soon as the ball is dead.

A time-out will be granted even if the opposition score a field goal, provided the request was made before the ball left the hands of the shooter. A time-out is charged to the coach of the team who made the request first and can only be withdrawn before the scorer signals to the officials.

Players are allowed to sit on the team bench during a time-out.

INJURIES

OFFICIALS CAN STOP THE GAME immediately to protect an injured player. If the injured player cannot continue to play within approximately 15 seconds, he must either be substituted or return within one minute. If free throws have been awarded to the injured player they must be taken by his substitute.

Players who are cut must leave the court immediately and only return when the bleeding has stopped and the wound has been securely covered. If an official is injured and cannot continue, the rest of the game will be handled by the other official on his own, unless a qualified substitute official is available.

EXTRA-TIME

IF A GAME is tied at the end of normal play, it will continue with a five-minute extra period or as many such periods as necessary to break the tie.

Injured players must leave the court immediately.

Playing Regulations

GAMES ARE STARTED by the referee, who tosses a jump ball vertically between two opposing players at the centre circle. The same procedure is followed at the beginning of each period played. Teams should always change baskets for the second half.

The ball becomes alive after reaching its highest point during a jump ball, when it is at the disposal of a free-throw shooter, and once it touches a player on the court following a

throw-in from out of bounds. It becomes dead at the end of a half (or period), after a goal, after an official's whistle or 30-second operator's signal has sounded, and when a free throw fails but is followed immediately by another free throw or a further penalty.

The ball is not dead at the whistle if it is in flight from a free throw.

JUMP, DEAD AND LIVE BALLS

AT THE TIME of a whistle, signal or end of period, the ball is not dead if it is in flight from a free throw or shot, or if a player is fouled while in the process of shooting after an

official's whistle has blown. Apart from starting play, a jump ball can be awarded when two players both have their hands on the ball and possession cannot be determined without undue roughness, and also when it is unclear which side was responsible for the ball going out of bounds. At a jump ball, the two jumpers stand in their own halves of the circle and are not allowed to tap the ball until it has started dropping towards them.

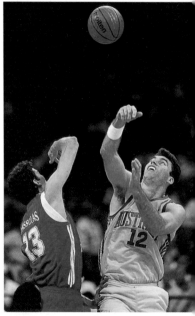

A jump ball.

Possession and Shooting

It is against the rules to hold the ball while running, to kick it deliberately with any part of the leg below the knee, or to fist it. A team is in control of the ball when one of its players is holding it while standing still, dribbling it or passing it to a team-mate. Team control ends when a player is dispossessed or when a shot is in progress.

A PLAYER IS judged to be in the act of shooting if he is attempting to throw, dunk or tap the ball towards the opponents' basket. The attempt continues until the ball has left the player's hand(s). In the case of an airborne shot, the attempt continues until the player's feet have returned to the ground. A foul can only be committed on a player in the act of shooting if the official decides that the player has begun the continuous movement of his shooting attempt.

A goal counts even if the ball has not left a player's hand(s) before a whistle blows, except at the end of a period or when the 30-second signal sounds. A player who taps a ball directly from a jump ball is not considered to be in the act of shooting.

Running with the ball is against the rules.

Team possession ends when the ball leaves the hands of the player attempting a shot.

Goals and Substitutions

A GOAL IS made when a live ball passes through the basket from above. A goal from a free throw is worth one point, while goals from the field count as either two or three points, depending on where the shot was taken from. If a team accidentally scores a field goal in its own basket, the points shall be recorded as scored by the captain of the opposing team. A three-point field goal becomes a two pointer if it is touched by another offensive or defensive player before entering the basket.

THROW-INS

AFTER CONCEDING a goal, a time-out or any other stoppage, a team must restart the game within five seconds of the ball being handed to one of their players on or behind the endline. Players should not move more than one step forwards or on to

A goal from a free throw is worth one point.

the court while throwing in, nor should they throw it over the backboard or attempt a direct shot at the basket. Any of these infringements will result in the opposition being given a throw-in from the same spot. No player should be within 1 m (3 ft) of the player making the throw-in.

Players are not allowed to step on to the court while throwing in.

SUBSTITUTIONS

BEFORE COMING ON COURT, a substitute should report to the scorer and be ready to play immediately once beckoned on by the official. The scorer indicates a substitution request by sounding his signal once the ball is dead, the game clock is stopped or the official has finished reporting a foul to the scorer's table. If the official thinks that any substitution has caused unreasonable delay, he can charge a time-out against the offending team. A substitution request can only be cancelled before the scorer's signal has sounded.

Termination of Play and Violations

The sounding of the timekeeper's signal indicates the end of a period, half or game. If a foul is committed as the timekeeper sounds his signal, any resulting free throws may be taken.

GAMES LOST BY FORFEIT OR DEFAULT

A TEAM FORFEITS a game if it refuses to play after being instructed to by the referee, if by its actions it prevents play

from taking place, if it is 15 minutes late on court, or if it is unable to field five players. A team defaults if it has fewer than two players on court during a game.

VIOLATIONS

THE PENALTY for a violation of the rules is loss of the ball by the offending team, with their opponents being awarded a throw-in from the nearest point to the violation.

A violation of the rules results in a throw-in being granted to the opposing team.

DRIBBLES

AFTER A PLAYER'S dribble has ended, the same player cannot begin a second dribble unless he has lost control because of shooting for goal, a tap by an opponent or a pass or fumble that has then touched another player. A player cannot throw the ball against the backboard and touch it again before it touches another player unless, in the official's opinion, it was a shot.

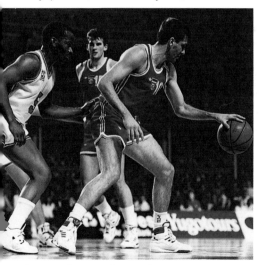

A player cannot begin a second dribble before another player has touched the ball or he has attempted a throw.

Specific Rules on the Court

TRAVEL RULE

A PIVOT OCCURS when a player who is holding a live ball steps once, or more than once, in any direction with the same foot while the other foot, called the pivot foot, stays in contact with the floor.

After establishing a pivot foot, it may be lifted only if the player is passing or trying for a field goal; it may not be lifted if the player is beginning a dribble before the ball is released from the hand(s).

Joe Wolf closely guarding Dino Radja.

THREE-SECOND RULE

WHILE HIS team has possession, a player cannot remain for more than three consecutive seconds in his opponents' restricted area. The three-second rule does not apply when the ball is in the air during a shot for goal, a rebound or when the ball is dead.

FIVE-SECOND RULE

A CLOSELY guarded player in possession must pass, shoot, roll or dribble the ball within five seconds.

10-SECOND RULE

WHEN A PLAYER gains control of a live ball in his back court, his team must take the ball into the front court within 10 seconds.

Once the ball is in the front court, the team in possession are not allowed to return it to the back court, even if they have a throw-in. A ball which has been deflected into the back court by a defending player may be recovered by either team.

Paul James of the Thames Valley Tigers, preparing his next move.

INTERFERENCE WITH THE BALL
ON OFFENCE AND DEFENCE

NEITHER AN offensive or defensive player can touch a shot when it is on its downward flight and yet above the level of the ring. This restriction ceases to apply when the ball touches the ring or it is obvious the ball will miss the ring.

A defensive player must not touch the ball or basket while the ball is within the basket, and neither a defensive or offensive player can touch the basket or backboard when a shot is in contact with the ring. If the violation is by the offence, no point can be scored and the opponents are awarded a throw-in. If it is by the defence, the shooter is awarded two or three points and the game is restarted from behind the endline.

A player cannot interfere with the ball on its downward flight above the level of the ring.

PRINCIPLE OF VERTICALITY

EACH PLAYER HAS the right to a position on court and the vertical position above him (a 'cylinder'). As soon as a player leaves his cylinder and makes body contact with an opponent who has not left his cylinder, that player is responsible for the contact. Players should not create additional space for themselves by using their arms.

LEGAL GUARDING POSITION

A DEFENSIVE player establishes a legal guarding position when he faces an opponent and has both feet on the floor in a normal straddle position. He is permitted to raise his arms above his head, but they must be within his cylinder.

Patrick Ewing in a legal guarding position.

PERSONAL FOULS

PERSONAL FOULS RESULTS from personal contact with an opponent or from unsporting behaviour. Basketball is theoretically a non-contact game, but personal contact cannot be avoided completely when 10 players are moving with great speed over a limited space. Even though it is each player's duty to avoid contact whenever possible, if the contact is accidental or the result of a genuine attempt to play the ball and does not place the opponent at a disadvantage, it need not be penalised.

A personal foul will be given against a player if he blocks, holds, charges, trips or impedes the progress of an opponent by extending his arm, shoulder, hip, knee or foot, if he bends his body into an abnormal position or uses rough tactics. If such a foul is committed on a player who is not in the act of shooting, his team will be awarded a throw-in. If it is committed on a player who is shooting

Fouls result from deliberate personal contact with another player.

and if the goal is made, it will count and a free throw will be awarded. If a shot for two points is unsuccessful, two free throws will be awarded, and if a shot for three points is unsuccessful three free throws will be awarded.

GUARDING A PLAYER WHO CONTROLS THE BALL

THE PLAYER HOLDING or dribbling the ball must be prepared to stop or change his direction whenever an opponent takes a legal guarding position in front of him. The defensive player, in turn, must avoid body contact before taking up his position and must not extend his arms, shoulders, hips or legs to prevent the dribbler from passing him. But he can move laterally or backwards to maintain the guarding position.

The player in possession of the ball must be prepared to move when the legal guarding position is established in front of him.

THE PLAYER WHO IS IN THE AIR

A PLAYER WHO has jumped from a spot on court has the right to land on the same spot. He can land on another spot provided that spot is not already occupied by an opponent, but an opponent cannot move into that path after the player has jumped into the air. Moving under a player is considered unsporting and can be a disqualifying foul.

Moving into another player's spot while he is in the air is considered unsporting.

GUARDING A PLAYER WHO
DOES NOT CONTROL THE BALL

A PLAYER WHO is not holding or dribbling the ball is entitled to move freely on the court and take any position not occupied by another player. The result of this is that a defensive player cannot move so close or so quickly and that an opponent does not have sufficient time or distance to stop or change direction.

SCREENING

LEGAL AND ILLEGAL screening occurs when a player attempts to delay or prevent an opponent who does not control the ball from reaching a desired position. It is legal if the player doing the screening is stationary inside his cylinder and has both feet on the floor when contact occurs. The screening is illegal if the player was moving when contact occurred.

If the screen is set outside a stationary opponent's field of vision, that opponent is allowed to take one normal step towards the screen without making contact. A player who is legally screened is responsible if there is any contact with the player who set up the screen.

Michael Jordan jumping within his cylinder.

PLAYING THE GAME

Tactics of the Game

Since the game was invented by Dr James Naismith back in 1891, basketball's rules have evolved and there have been some fundamental changes, but it remains essentially the same simple game.

THE OBJECTIVE OF the game is for a team to score goals in the opposition's basket and prevent them from doing the same. The basic tactic reiterated by all coaches throughout the last 100 years or so is: keep possession of the ball as much as possible – if the other team doesn't have the ball, they can't score.

Naismith saw the game of basketball as one based on skill rather than physical power. Today, skill is absolutely vital, but most of the

The main object of the game is to score goals in the opposition's basket.

top players are also robust and almost all are above average height. But Alton Byrd, who had a superb career in Britain when he moved from the NBL, was slightly built and only 1.7 m (5 ft 8 in) tall, and managed to reach the top of the game, through skill and amazing speed of mind.

The maximum number of players allowed on court for one team is now five. The early rules did not stipulate playing numbers – Naismith suggested that between three and 40 could play. It would be interesting to review the tactics employed by a coach during a 40-a-side basketball match in those early years.

Alton Byrd who, despite his stature, reached the top of the game.

Developing Tactics

TEAM TACTICS

THE MODERN GAME of basketball is fast and furious, with astonishing speed of movement and passing. But when a team huddles around a coach whether for an NBA or school match, the coach will issue a range of instructions dealing with the strength and weaknesses of the opposition and will no doubt add one rider: make sure you keep the ball away from the other team.

The agreed pre-match tactics of a team will be based on knowledge of the opposition's strengths and weaknesses. However, unforeseen incidents can happen during a match and a game plan may have to be radically altered in response to changing circumstances – such as an injury to a team member or the opposition suddenly introducing players much taller than your own.

All five of the players starting a match can be substituted and the players on the bench are often called upon by the coach if he wants to change his formation on the court or if he requires a substitute to carry out a specific task – maybe man-marking an opposition player who is playing well and finding too much space.

Coach discussing team tactics with his players.

The Spurs vs. the Sonics in 1998.

SCORING TACTICS

THERE ARE USUALLY many points scored in a basketball match, unlike games such as soccer when just one goal can win a game.

Basketball is about resilience and it must be remembered that a team can score 100 points and still lose. Most teams look to play a percentage game and, apart from keeping possession, will want to cut down the number of errors made.

When attacking, always aim to shoot from the best possible position – the long-range shot looks spectacular if it is successful, but is usually made after an attack has failed to get close to the basket. Long-range shooters are also more likely to miss their target than players close to the basket.

When defending, the object is to restrict the opposition's shooting options and keep them as far away from the basket as possible.

When devising tactics for your team, look at the professionals and assess their tactical play. They may be fitter and have better skills than players in your team, but even they must follow the basic rule to win – that is, score more points than the opposition.

Playing a shot close to the basket is more likely to be successful than taking a long shot.

The aim when defending is to restrict the opponent's opportunities of scoring.

Positions

NAMES OF POSITIONS

There are three basic playing positions in the game of basketball: guard, forward and centre. However, basketball is a game in which there are few restrictions on playing positions. Each player is free to occupy any area of the court, receive the ball and shoot from any position.

GUARD

THE GUARD IS usually one of the smallest and quickest players in the team and tends to operate farthest away from the opposing basket. When his side are on the attack, he will operate in the area of the court between the centre line and the free throw line extended to the side lines.

He will be responsible for fetching the ball up court to initiate attacks. A top-rated guard will push in close to the basket to draw the defence and then pass to a team-mate in a better position to shoot. Guards are also usually proficient with long-range shots and driving to the basket. Accuracy in passing the ball is also essential for a player in this position.

Guards are usually best at long-range shots at goal.

FORWARD

AS THEIR NAME suggests, forwards are the attacking focus of a team, and play in the area of the court between the restricted area and the side lines. They are inevitably among the tallest players of the team and must be able to shoot well – from both the corner and side of the court. Forwards should also be able to fight for possession at rebounds if a shot is missed or blocked.

The position of forward involves more attacking play.

The centre tends to stay near the opposition's basket, making close-range shots at goal.

CENTRE

THE CENTRE is usually the tallest player in the side and plays in attack near to the opposition's basket. A good centre should be able to shoot well, close to the basket – and also perform well under pressure from covering defenders.

He should also be able to make his own space to receive a pass. But most crucial of all, he should be able to make the most of any rebounds close to the basket. The centre is also known as a 'post' or 'pivot' player.

TEAM ON COURT

THE NUMBER OF guards, forwards and centres on court at any given time will depend on the state of the match and the coach's tactics. Most teams favour a 1-2-2 (one guard, two centres and two forwards) or 2-1-2 (two guards, one centre and two forwards) line-up.

Although a basketball player will line up nominally as a guard, centre or forward, the game requires each man to attack and defend at all times. When your team has possession it is your job to support the attack on the opposition's basket and be prepared to pass, receive the ball or shoot at every opportunity. When the other side has the ball you must defend your basket. The court is a relatively small area, but throughout a match you will have to cover a great deal of floor space.

Despite holding a nominal position, all players must be able to attack and defend as required.

Passing

Passing is by far the most effective way of moving the ball around the court. A good pass in basketball will not see the ball in the air for too long – a hanging ball will give more time for your opponents to intercept it and gain possession.

PLEASE NOTE, however, safe passing will always please the coach. The spectacular long pass that travels the length of the court – which is often referred to as the 'javelin' or 'baseball' pass – will look good if a team-mate gathers the ball and puts it in the net, but far too often it can lead to your side losing possession.

Passing the ball is the best way of moving it around the court.

HOW TO PASS

THE MOST productive passes are short-range, made to a team-mate who is attacking the opposition's net, and reach the receiver when and where he wants it.

Keep it simple. In most cases your passes should be no more than 4.5 m (13 ft) in length. However, if you see a team-mate standing unguarded near the basket, by all means try the long pass.

When attempting to make any pass, the key points to remember are to know exactly where the intended receiver is on the court.

Always know where your receiver is before passing the ball.

PASSING TECHNIQUES

TRY TO BE deceptive and always keep your opponents
guessing as to where and when you are about to pass the ball.
Don't stare at the team-mate you are about to pass to and try
to avoid 'winding up' your pass, as this again will give the
opposition time to cover the move.

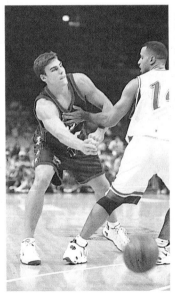

The great
players always
disguise their
intentions, and it is
often said that the
superstars of the
sport, such as
Michael Jordan, are
so good at hiding
their intentions
that at times they
confuse even their
own team-mates by
the speed and
inventiveness of
their passing.

Once you have
made the pass,
don't relax – always
keep moving on
the court and find

*Try and surprise
your opponents with
the type of pass you
make with the ball.*

space to support the man with the ball. Be prepared at all times to take a return pass or other pass later in the move.

Always watch the man with the ball and position yourself to his best advantage.

Types of Passing

There are four basic passing techniques: the chest; overhead; bounce; and hand-off pass.

CHEST PASS

THIS IS THE most common and perhaps most important pass in basketball. It is used for fast, accurate passing at short range when there is no defender between you and your team-mate.

The chest pass is made from a position with the ball in both hands, with the fingers alongside the ball and thumbs behind.

The pass is made by extending the arms and pushing the ball away with the fingers. As the pass is made, the whole body moves forward to help deliver the ball. When the ball has been released, the fingers should be pointing in the direction of the throw.

The receiving player should help the passer – indicating where he wants the ball delivered by extending his hand. It will usually be the hand farthest away from the defender, and it to this arm that the passer should attempt to deliver the ball.

Chest Pass

Extend the arms

Push ball away with fingers

Point fingers in direction of throw

Move body forward to help deliver ball

OVERHEAD PASS

THIS IS A pass favoured by taller players who wish to bypass the opposition's smaller players. The ball is held in both hands above the head and a snap of the wrists and fingers should direct it to a team-mate over an opponent. The ball should be kept in front of the head using the wrists and forearms for power.

Hold ball above head with both hands

Flight of ball over head of opponent

Snap wrists and fingers to release ball

Overhead Pass

BOUNCE PASS

THIS HELPS A player pass the ball under a taller opponent or a player with his arms held high. The pass is similar to the chest pass, except the ball is delivered from a lower position (level with the hip) and the ball reaches a team-mate after being skidded via the floor.

The bounce pass is usually made with just one hand. It should be made at speed and to a team-mate not too far away from you. There is a real danger that the bounce pass will be intercepted unless it is executed quickly and accurately.

Bounce Pass

Move round opposing player to pass ball

Deliver ball from hip level

Make pass with one hand

Ball skids along floor (note speed of ball)

HAND-OFF PASS

A SHORT hand-off pass is executed when a team-mate is cutting close to the ball handler. The ball is knocked into the air so that the cutting player can take it immediately it has left the passer's hand.

Dribbling

THE DRIBBLE IS one of the most important and essential skills in basketball. It allows the player to move forward with the ball, and a good dribbler is hard to dispossess. Always remember, however, basketball is a team game, and if you have the ball, always look for a team-mate who may be in a better scoring position than yourself. A simple pass that leads to a team-mate scoring is better than a complex – albeit spectacular – dribble and will impress the coach, team-mates and ultimately the team's supporters more than an elaborate dribble that comes to nothing.

HOW TO DRIBBLE

EVERY PLAYER IN a team should be able to dribble and be prepared to devote time to improving their skills. Dribbling is

carried out with the fingers and pads of the hand – not the palm. The ball should be pushed down firmly, with the wrist playing a major part of the action.

Inexperienced players bounce the ball too far in front of them and this just gives the opposition players time to dispossess them. Practise bouncing the ball

Being able to dribble effectively is an essential skill in basketball.

without keeping your eye on it: the top players are able to dribble the ball and to look up to assess what passing or shooting opportunities are unfolding at the same time.

Always ensure that only one hand comes in contact with the ball when dribbling. If both hands touch the ball the dribble is deemed to be over. Good players keep the ball between knee and waist height when dribbling and alternate controlling the ball between right and left hand.

It is no good if you can dribble with just one hand, the opposition will soon spot the weakness and make you pay for it.

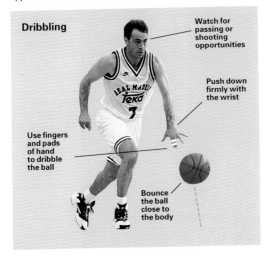

Dribbling

Watch for passing or shooting opportunities

Push down firmly with the wrist

Use fingers and pads of hand to dribble the ball

Bounce the ball close to the body

Shooting

MANY SEE SHOOTING as the most glamorous and exciting of all the basketball skills. It is true that if you can't get the ball in the basket you are not going to win your match. However, it must be stressed that all the skills are equally important

and while it makes sense for a younger player to spend time improving his shooting ability, he must not forget to practise the other skills such as passing and dribbling. There are five types of shots: the set shot, the lay-up shot, the jump shot, the free-throw shot and the close-up shot.

There are many different types of shot that can be used in a match.

THE SET SHOT

THE SET SHOT is taken when there is an opponent between you and the basket, but he is too far away to impede you. A player must get his stance right for this shot, which means the feet pointing in the same direction as the shot and the shoulders facing squarely to the basket. The player will look at the basket throughout the shot. The ball is held in both hands but the shot is made with one hand – the non-shooting hand supports the ball at the side. The movement of the shot starts with a powerful drive with the legs and the player will be at full stretch when he releases the ball and should follow through with a snap of the wrist and fingers.

THE LAY-UP SHOT

THIS IS USUALLY taken on the run and is one of the most
frequently used methods of scoring. The player dribbles
towards the basket and then jumps up and at the basket. He will
attempt to shoot the ball off the backboard and into the basket.
He will stretch and try to release the ball as close to the basket as
possible. You must remember that once you have the ball in
both hands after dribbling you can only take two steps – so step
two should be your take-off step.

Keep eyes on the basket

Take the ball in both hands

Take off from Step Two

Step One

Lay-up Shot

JUMP SHOT

THE JUMP SHOT is perhaps the most effective shot in basketball. It is made in the same way as the set shot, but the ball is delivered while the player is jumping. It is an option if a defender is in your way and you can make space for the shot by jumping. The player will attempt to take off with both feet and jump vertically. The ball is taken to a position above the head and released near the top of the jump with an upward extension of the arm. Some inexperienced players may find the jump shot difficult to execute and it is wise not to use it until the set shot has been mastered.

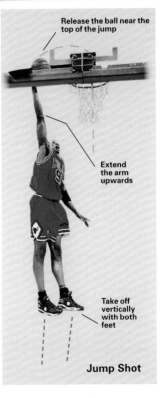

Release the ball near the top of the jump

Extend the arm upwards

Take off vertically with both feet

Jump Shot

FREE-THROW SHOT

THE FREE-THROW shot is very similar to the set shot and is awarded after a foul has been committed. A player has to stand with his feet behind the free-throw line and no other player can impede or prevent him from throwing at the basket. The only thing a player has to do with a free-throw is get the ball in the basket. The technique for the free-throw shot is the same as the set-shot. It is likely that every member of a team will have to make a free-throw shot during a match, so it is vital that you practise this type of shot.

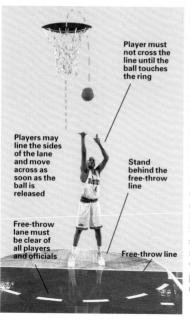

Player must not cross the line until the ball touches the ring

Players may line the sides of the lane and move across as soon as the ball is released

Stand behind the free-throw line

Free-throw lane must be clear of all players and officials

Free-throw line

CLOSE-UP SHOT

THERE WILL BE times when a player is close to the basket and none of the previously described shots can be used. One of the most common close-up shots is the dunk. This is when a player jumps high and throws (or dunks) the ball down in the basket. It is a spectacular way of scoring, but is very difficult to execute as the basket is 3.05 m (10 ft) off the ground.

Another type of close-up shot is the hook shot. This is usually made when a player receives the ball with his back to the basket. The player then pivots and jumps to make the shot. It is not a powerful shot and the shooter would have put some backspin on the ball for when it hits the ring or backboard.

England's Steve Bucknall demonstrating a dunk.

Offence

TO WIN A basketball match a team must score more points than the opposition and that means getting the ball into the basket as often as possible. No points are awarded for style or interpretation and there are fewer controversial decisions to be made by the match officials that could affect the outcome than in most other sports. The result of the match is literally in the hands of the team's five players on the court.

POSSESSION OF THE BALL

WHEN AN opposition attack breaks down and your team gains possession, your task is to get either yourself or a team-mate in the best possible shooting position to put the ball in the basket.

As soon as you get the ball, you

The Bulls vs. the Pacers.

should quickly consider the alternatives available to you. You can pass, drive, shoot or move with the ball. As a team, you should try and spread out on the court to make it difficult for one defender to look after two attackers.

Try changing your attacking formation to confuse the opposition into drawing defenders away from the under-basket area. If there is space, ensure that you or a team-mate is free in the under-basket area.

If there is no chance of a successful fast break out of defence, alter the tempo of the attack. Sometimes a slow build-up can be more successful than tearing down the court at breakneck speed and finding yourself going nowhere.

Attacking play during the men's national basketball final in Sheffield.

Offensive Techniques

LIKE MOST ASPECTS of basketball, attack should be a simple operation. The Dream Team at the 1992 Olympics in Barcelona captivated all and sundry with the speed and brilliance of their attacking movements. In reality, their attacks were like most others, but they were carried out at breathtaking pace, in terms of physical motion and speed of thought. When they gained possession, a player checked his options and made his move, and usually within a single pass or so, the ball was in the basket. But they stuck to the basic attacking play in basketball, which is to pass to a team-mate and move towards

The United States Dream Team, Barcelona, 1992.

the basket. They slowed the game down at times and rapid changes of pace and brilliant ball-handling made them a great attacking team.

'Magic' Johnson of the Los Angeles Lakers, demonstrating speed of mind and action.

One of the most common errors made by a player new to basketball is to play too quickly, especially when attacking. As the Dream Team showed, speed of mind is sometimes as important as quick legs.

A good defender will have assessed your strengths and weaknesses as an attacker. Do likewise and try to discover shortcomings in his defensive game.

Other simple things to remember about attacking are always try and face the basket and attempt to pass ahead. Beware of team-mates on attack getting into difficulty and try to support them. At all times, try to stop committing the cardinal sin of losing possession. If you do, you are immediately back in defensive mode.

Defence

THE BASIC RULE of defensive play is to try and keep the ball away from the opposition as much as possible. However, when your team has lost possession you must think immediately of defending your basket. Always be alert in defence and make life as difficult as possible for your opponent without making contact. Support your team-mates and look to cover for a member of your team if he has been beaten.

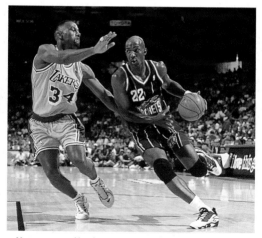

Use your arms and hands to prevent an attacker from passing or shooting.

DEFENDING

USE YOUR BODY as a shield when confronting an attacker, but try not to touch him and concede a foul. Your hands and arms should also be used to stop an attacker attempting to dribble, pass or shoot.

When defending against a shooter, you should try and anticipate the timing of his shot and don't jump too soon in an attempt to block his effort – a good player will shape up to shoot in the hope of the defender reacting too soon and then make another move having sold the dummy to the defending player. The same basic rules apply when defending against a player who is about to make a pass to an attacking colleague – always try to guess what an attacking player is about to do but make sure you time your intervention perfectly. Look to pressurise the man with the ball and force him into errors.

Time your jump carefully when defending against the shooter.

Defensive Techniques

A GOOD DEFENDER will know the strengths and weaknesses of his opponent and play to them. For example, if an attacker is a brilliant left-handed dribbler, try to position yourself to his left to restrict his movements on that side.

Once a team has lost possession, all five players on the court immediately become defenders. In basketball, every player is expected to have all the skills to defend and attack as one unit.

As when attacking, a good defensive team will try to play a percentage game. Manoeuvre an attacker into the least favourable shooting or dribbling position and certainly keep the shooter as far away from the basket as possible.

MARKING

MAN-TO-MAN marking is a simple defensive ploy. This involves a defender marking a specific opponent, regardless of where

A team should defend and attack as a unit.

he moves on the court. In this case, the defender keeps his eye on the attacker and not the ball.

In a zone defence, all five players on court work as a unit and respond to the ball. Each player is responsible for the area of the court in which he is positioned.

DEFENSIVE FORMATIONS

DEFENCES SHOULD BE quick to adapt and change their formation to mirror that of the attacking side, who will be looking for space and aiming to draw defenders from the under-basket area.

Understanding your team's tactics, and especially the movements of team-mates, requires constant and clear communication between defenders. Keep talking to the other members of your team to ensure you have your defensive respon-sibilities sorted out.

When using man-to-man marking, always keep your eye on the player rather than the ball.

VARIATIONS OF THE GAME

Varieties of Basketball

The massive popularity of basketball has meant players of all ages are keen to play, practise and train for the sheer love of the sport on any court, playground or open space they can find. Pick-up basketball is the term given to games that are apparently spontaneous and start anywhere there is a basket, a ball and willing players.

TRAINING ROUTINES have led to the emergence of a number of variations of the conventional game, including one-on-one and three-on-three encounters. The latter form,

Street basketball in California.

which features three-man teams, has proved so popular that it has become established at competitive level, with national championships and even a world tour held under the auspices of the NBA. Many cities in the United States have league and tournaments devoted to this form of basketball. Various shooting competitions and championships have been held featuring teams or individuals.

Those confined to wheelchairs are not denied the pleasure of taking part, as wheelchair basketball has developed into a well-organised sport throughout the world. Apart from those with sensory disabilities, wheelchair basketball is played by paraplegics and amputees, plus those suffering from cerebral palsy and polio.

Wheelchair basketball offers nearly all physically disabled people the chance to participate and compete on equal terms.

A number of initiatives have been created by basketball governing bodies throughout the world to encourage children and young people to take up the sport.

Mini basketball, aimed at the nine-to-12 age bracket, is more or less based on the conventional game. The main differences are that the basket is lower from the ground and the ball is smaller in mini basketball.

Three-on-Three Basketball

Three-on-three basketball developed as a training
exercise, but is now played as a competitive game.
It takes place on only one half of the court and there
is only one basket to shoot into.

T WO THREE-MAN teams line up and in competition the
winners are the side to reach 15 points, with at least a two-
point lead.
However, the
required winning
total can vary,
especially in
informal games.
The duration of
the game can also
differ but is usually
10 or 15 minutes.

The question of
who has possession
at the start of a
match is decided
by the captains
tossing a coin. The
match starts from
out-of-bounds on

*Three-on-three
basketball being played
in the US.*

the side line and possession changes sides after each successful goal, violation of the rules and defensive rebound.

Apart from shooting fouls, the team gaining possession after a foul takes the ball out-of-bounds opposite the top of the three-point line before starting their attack.

If a foul is committed on a player who is in the act of shooting, an additional free throw is awarded. Whether or not the shooter is successful with his free throw, the defence regains possession.

If a foul is made on a shooter and the basket is missed, a free throw is given. If the free throw is successful, possession is passed to the defence. If the free throw is missed, the attacking side keeps the ball.

The winners in three-on-three basketball are the first team to reach 15 points with a two-point lead.

Pick-up or Outdoor Basketball

There is no governing body for pick-up or any impromptu outdoor game of basketball and a formal set of rules simply doesn't exist. The customs and rules have evolved from the countless pick-up games played throughout the world by spontaneously formed teams over the years.

NO RULE BOOK has been written, but there has emerged a culture around the game that sees its participants adhere to a uniform set of rules and even fashion – as seen in the film *White Men Can't Jump*.

There are no match officials in pick-up basketball and every issue, from who touched the ball to the current score, is contended.

The first team to score 11, 15 or 21 baskets wins. Most teams prefer to play to 21 but if there are pressures of time or other teams waiting to use the court, the

There are no formal rules for outdoor or pick-up basketball, but an accepted set of rules is generally adhered to.

lower numbers are accepted as winning totals. Each basket is worth one point.

If the score is level at 10-10, 14-14, or 20-20, a side must score two straight baskets to win the match.

With no match officials overseeing the game and no hard-and-fast set of rules, a player who has been fouled has to 'call his own foul' to claim the infringement.

Pick-up games played on a half court are called 'winners' or 'possession' matches. The team that scores a basket keeps possession, which means a team must play defensively otherwise it will never see the ball. In these games, if possession changes sides via a rebound or turnover the cry of 'take it back' can be heard. This requires the player who now has the ball to take it back to an agreed point before they can begin their attack.

There are no officials in street basketball, and a player is allowed to call his own foul.

Wheelchair Basketball

Wheelchair basketball is played on regular courts, although the various leagues have their own rulebook. Many of the regulations applying to the conventional game are used in wheelchair basketball.

T HE REGULATIONS relating to the three-second rule apply more or less to wheelchair basketball, other than the fact that the time is extended to either four or five seconds depending on which rules are being followed.

Jump balls are used only at the start of each half. In other jump ball situations, teams will alternate possession and restart the match with a throw-in from out-of-bounds.

A dribble can be made in two ways. Firstly, by wheeling the chair forward or backwards with two pushes and bouncing the ball simultaneously on the floor (just as a player runs and bounces the ball in regular basketball). The other method of dribbling allowed is to wheel the chair with two pushes followed by one or more taps on the floor with the ball, after which the player may start pushing again.

Players can push their chairs with one or two hands, in any direction. Taking more than two pushes in succession constitutes a travelling violation and the ball is awarded to the other side.

The location of a player is determined by where any part of his chair is touching the floor. This rule is used to decide whether or not a player is in-bounds.

Many of the conventional rules of the game apply to wheelchair matches.

Mini Basketball

In mini basketball, lower baskets and smaller basketballs are used, and the game is divided into four playing periods of 10 minutes. Each member of the side must play at least one period and no player is allowed to play in all of the first three periods.

S UBSTITUTIONS ARE not allowed except between periods. There are no 30-second rules, three-point rules, team foul rules or time-outs.

The basic rules and regulations of conventional basketball have evolved slowly over the years and most of the variations of the sport stick quite rigidly to the main concept of the sport. The unchanging rule in all variations is that the side scoring the most points wins the match.

The Greater London Leopards playing the Manchester Giants.

COMPENDIUM
Glossary

Airball: A shot by a player that completely misses the basket.

Assist: A pass given to a receiver that results in a score.

Back court: The half of the court containing a team's basket.

Bankshot: A shot that uses the backboard.

Barnstorming: Term that originated in North America; it describes teams that travelled out of necessity to reach commercially viable audiences.

Baseline (or endline): The line at each end of the court that marks the start of the out-of-bounds area.

Block: Illegal personal contact by a player on an opponent.

Breakaway: A play when a player steals the ball close to his own basket and races the length of the court to score.

Centre: Position often taken by the tallest player in a team. Scores from in-close, block shots and rebounds.

Dunk: To score a basket by jumping with the ball above the net and forcing it down through the net. Also known as a 'slam dunk' or a 'stuff'.

Fast break: To move rapidly out of defence after gaining possession to set up an attack before the opposition has reformed its own defence.

Field goal: A scoring shot from open play made from inside or outside the three-point arc. It is worth two or three points.

Five-second rule: A player in possession must pass, dribble or shoot within five seconds of getting the ball.

Forward: One of the player positions. A team usually has two forwards and they play predominantly in the front court, normally between the sidelines and restricted area. They are usually tall and their job is to rebound, shoot for basket and provide support for the centre inside.

Free throws: A throw at the basket without any interference from the opposition. Awarded for fouls – personal or technical. Taken from the free-throw line, a successful throw is worth one point.

Front court: The half of the court that contains the opposing side's basket, and where your team attacks.

Guards: One of the player positions. Usually smaller than the forwards, they are the primary ball-handlers and will be good dribblers and passers. They will also be good shooters from distance.

Hack: Slang term for an aggressive foul.

Held ball: When two or more players have one or both hands firmly on the ball at the same time and both teams claim possession. Play is stopped and starts again with a jump ball.

Javelin pass: A single-handed, overhead pass.

Jump ball: A method of putting the ball into play. A match official throws the ball up between two opposing players who battle for possession.

MVP: Most Valuable Player, an accolade awarded to players after a game or tournament.

Out-of-bounds: Players are deemed out-of-bounds if they touch the floor or stray on or outside the boundary lines.

Overtime: A five-minute session that is played when a game ends with the scores level.

Personal foul: A violation committed by an active player, that involves illegal contact with an opponent when the ball is live.

Point guard: Often the guard with the best handling skills and who usually directs the offensive play of his team.

Rebound (offensive or defensive): The retrieval of a misplaced shot by an attacking or defending player.

Rookie: Term applied to a new member of a team.

calling excessive time-outs and even hanging on the rim of the basket.

10-second rule: Having gained possession, a team must advance over the half-way line within 10 seconds.

Three-point basket: A successful shot made from outside the three-point arc. It is worth three points.

Sideline: The line running down each side of the court marking the out-of-bounds area.

Strong side: The side of the court (right or left) where the ball is currently located.

Technical foul: A foul by any player or member of a team's coaching staff that does not involve contact with a player. Technical fouls include un-sportsmanlike behaviour,

Time-out: A stoppage of play for a designated time. Coaches may request two time-outs per half, lasting up to a minute, during which they discuss strategy with their players. The NBA allows seven time-outs per game.

Turnover: When an attacking side loses the ball without taking a shot.

Weak side: The side of the court (right or left) opposite to where the ball is currently located.

Useful Addresses and Numbers

**English Basketball
Association (EBBA)**
48 Bradford Road
Stanningley
Leeds LS28 6DF
Tel: 0113 236 1166

**The Basketball League
Limited**
The Lodge
Castle Bromwich Hall
Chester Road
Castle Bromwich
Birmingham B36 9DE
Tel: 0121 749 1355

**Basketball Association
of Wales**
Connies House
Rhymney River Bridge Road
Cardiff CF3 7YZ
Tel: 01222 506715

Irish Basketball Association
National Basketball Arena
Tymon Park
Dublin 24
Republic of Ireland
Tel: 003531 459 0211

**Scottish Basketball
Association**
Caledonia House
South Gyle
Edinburgh EH12 9DQ
Tel: 0131 317 7260

**National Basketball
Association (NBA)**
Olympic Tower
645 Fifth Avenue
New York
NY 10022, USA
Tel: 001 212 688 9622

**International Basketball
Federation (FIBA)**
Boschetsrieder Strasse 67
D-81379 Munich
Germany
Tel: 0049 897 481 580

Bibliography

The Ultimate Encyclopaedia of Basketball: The Definitive Illustrated Guide to the NBA by Ron Smith (Hodder & Stoughton).

The European Basketball Register by Dan Peterson (Libreria Dello Sport).

Play the Game – Basketball by David Titmuss (Ward Lock).

FIBA Basketball, editor Rob Dugdale (Alliance International Media Limited). Official publication of the International Basketball Federation. Monthly magazine.

XXL Basketball, editor Lee Berry (Alliance International Media Limited). Monthly magazine featuring the NBA.

Basketball League: Official Handbook (Basketball League Limited). Published annually.

Index